SIZE DOESN'T MATTER

Why Small Business Is Big Business
Profit Now from the Small Business Boom!

Jeff Shavitz

Published by Happy About®, a THiNKaha® imprint
20660 Stevens Creek Blvd., Suite 210, Cupertino, CA 95014
http://happyabout.com

First Printing: August, 2015
Paperback ISBN: 978-1-60005-260-6 (1-60005-260-6)
eBook ISBN: 978-1-60005-261-3 (1-60005-261-4)
Place of Publication: Silicon Valley, California, USA
Library of Congress Number: 2015946450

Trademarks

Warning and Disclaimer

This book is dedicated to the world of small business owners and entrepreneurs who collectively drive the entire world economy.

This book is also lovingly dedicated to my family—Jill, Jennifer, Lexi, and Andrew— who mean the world to me.

In the 1748 essay "Advice to a Young Tradesman," Benjamin Franklin made the famous, insightful, and often-quoted statement, "Time is money."

Considering this premise, I chose to designate each chapter in this book as a time of day. This felt more appropriate to me than the word "chapter" since, as the ever-insightful Ben so wisely said, time *is* indeed money—especially for the entrepreneur and small business owner.

Contents

Introducing Jeff Shavitz: Not Famous . . . Yet

> "I've always been famous,
> it's just no one knew it yet."
>
> —LADY GAGA, SINGER

I realize there are literally hundreds of books currently on the market offering advice about running a small business. Okay, more like thousands. I'm no mind reader here, but I'm going to guess that you're probably thinking, *So why write another one?*

I understand. There are certainly plenty of books about the entrepreneurial traits necessary to create your successful venture. Maybe you first saw this book on the web through some pop-up link that hit your screen. I might have implored you to buy it from Amazon. You could be a friend or family member I managed to "guilt" into buying it. However it is that you found *Size Doesn't Matter*, I knew going in you'd most likely think, as I often do, *The world doesn't need any more books on this topic.*

Am I right?

The Fortune 500 CEOs of multibillion-dollar companies who usually write or are featured in the books, motivational DVDs, and magazines already out there certainly have more experience and fame than I do. That's why you probably also wondered what qualifies me—an essentially unknown first-time author—to share my story and insights about business in a book.

Bear with me: I think I will quickly dispel any doubts you might have. The reason for my confidence is actually very simple. I bring a unique combination of experience to the table that most of those other books don't have: I'm an expert at starting and running small and very small businesses—let's call them SBs to save some words. I also work with SB owners every day.

There really aren't many people writing books today who have this level of experience to share.

Between you and me (we're alone here—right?), the process of running those huge, well-established companies we always read about everywhere isn't close to what's required to manage a small business or to launch a start-up venture.

Are you launching a new mega corporation? No? In all those other books and DVDs, how much of the information do you suppose directly applies to what you really need to know to launch, build, or work within an SB?

I think maybe it's time you had access to someone who's had extensive experience digging in the same trench you're preparing to dig. I think you need to hear the real story from someone who's still there digging today. Most of the famous CEOs and mega titans we read about have never experienced launching or working within an SB. If they have, it was decades ago.

When it comes to start-ups, I've done it three times—with different levels of success. SBs? I'm involved with them now.

My clients today are also all entrepreneurs with their own businesses of all sizes.

It gets better.

In addition to placating my entrepreneurial spirit over the past twenty-five-plus years, I've also experienced large corporate America—from the inside—when I worked in the investment banking division of Lehman Brothers for a period of time.

I think Lehman qualifies as a Fortune 500 company—in its day, anyway. I used to enjoy a personal fantasy that leaving the analyst position I took in 1988 (my first job after college) would eventually lead to the demise of that enormous institution. It didn't, but I still like to pretend it did!

I believe this corporate America experience, coupled with my extensive involvement with multiple small businesses, provides me with a truly unique set of skills and expertise to share. I also believe these skills and expertise are what you need as you enter into any SBs at any level.

I might just be the one unique voice out there, providing you with access to a very rare in-depth understanding of how both sides of the spectrum operate. Even better, I can also show you how each business type fails to operate efficiently. This is stuff only I could share. Stuff you better know going in if you want to avoid the mistakes I made along the way to where you're headed.

I'm not asking you to take my word for it, either. I'll delve more in depth into my various business experiences—on both sides of the fence—during the time we spend together here. I'm more interested right now in making sure our time extends beyond the first chapter. I'm also guilty of just reading the first chapter of many books—so I'm hoping you'll keep reading a bit more to you see for yourself the value I have to offer.

You'll find that some of the recollections I've gathered to share with you here are downright funny; others are simply strange. Some are confrontational; others involve moral dilemmas, family issues, financial extremes, and many emotional days of unbelievable ups and downs.

All these experiences are extremely important educational steps in my own development as an entrepreneur. It's my hope that, by sharing them, you'll see you're not alone as you weave your way through the enigmatic maze of business.

As I said, I think you'll find that this book is truly unique, one that had to be written. It definitely won't be boring.

How Time Flies

I didn't break this book up into chapters. Instead I decided to go with chapters that signify the hours in a day because time most certainly is money in the entrepreneur's world.

I said you'll find this is a truly unique book. It starts with the chapter headings and doesn't stop there! But wait—there's another reason behind those clocks that start out each chapter. It also signifies the thought process behind building or working within an SB. It's completely different from the kind of thinking required to thrive in a Lehman Brothers–type corporate environment. It has nothing to do with long or short hours, but there's no clocking out and going home at the end of the day as an entrepreneur. You can't succeed without taking responsibility and running with it full-bore. Sometimes, the days simply don't end, running into one another as you pull one all-nighter after another.

Even when you do go home to enjoy some "normal" family

time or partake in some nonbusiness activities to "get your balance on," the entrepreneur's brain doesn't stop working. I know mine never does—even when I'm sleeping.

At work or at home, watching your daughter's high school play or out fishing, awake or asleep—you'll find your mind keeps on churning, working through recent problems, turning over new ideas, and reexamining old ones.

You'll discover, as you get more involved with your own SB or working within one, it tends to take over everything you do. Your mind is no different . . . but the thinking itself is a lot different from working for a corporate behemoth. There you might have long days, but you can still clock out at the end of the day, go home, and not think about it again until you clock back in the next morning.

To better illustrate this concept, it seemed to me that twenty-four chapters, each identified by a time of a day, would do it. Still, like any entrepreneur, twenty-four hours wasn't enough to finish. Fortunately or unfortunately, you'll also see the clock start indicating 11:30 p.m., 11:45 p.m., and 11:55 p.m., as we speed up the thinking to get the book finished by midnight.

Yes . . . this, too, is how the entrepreneur must really be ready to operate—even when there aren't enough hours in the day to get everything done.

If nothing else, I wrote this book because I want you to see I'm also just like you. I'm an entrepreneur myself. I wake up in the middle of night with "an issue" that I just can't get off my mind so I can fall back asleep. I hate when that happens, but it happens often. The worst is when I check my iPhone on my daily 3:30 a.m. trip to the bathroom and find myself shouting a hearty, "SHIT!" to myself when I read the email that came in after-hours.

That gets my mind racing, and then there's no way I'm falling back asleep.

In my defense—I know I should never check my phone in the middle of the night, but I suppose I'll never learn. Besides, it's still such a rush having an incoming email or text waiting for me. For some reason, I feel like a loser if nobody sends me an email when I power on, even if I erupt in colorful language when I see it.

Call it a curse. For me, it comes with the territory. I think you'll discover it does with you, too.

The point: being a small business owner or key employee, I know how important small business is to the overall economy. I understand the odds every entrepreneur faces daily, and there's a vast array of unique experiences and lessons I can share with you.

I'm also now a first-time author (if you can really call me that). That's a new thing for me. I actually wrote this book as much for myself—to share my story with my family and three children—as I did for the rest of the world. My children make fun of me for writing a book because I can barely help them get through their high school English classes. But there's always a first time for everything!

I'm hopeful this book will challenge you to think differently, to think of new concepts. I want to push you to success as an entrepreneur.

Side Note: To assist you, I've also included a few blank pages at the back of the book for note-taking. This serves two purposes: 1) It makes the book longer, and 2) It provides an easy place for you to quickly jot down key thoughts as you read.

Overall, I want this to be a fun, possibly even provocative, read. My challenge to you is to identify at least ten "action points" that you'll be able to jump on within ten days of reading this book. I call this the "10 and 10!" The real-life stories and vignettes I'll be sharing should spark thoughts on your current business or the new business you plan to start or re-create. Please use the blank pages in the back to help you push the envelope. Think differently about your business, and it will become a reality.

I also hope you'll make use of technology and social media. Visit me at www.jeffshavitz.com where you can tweet me, email me, or link in with me on LinkedIn to share your comments and stories about your own journey. I want to learn from you, too.

2:00 A.M.

The Joy of Hangin' Out

> "All humans are entrepreneurs not because they should start companies, but because the will to create is encoded in human DNA."
>
> —REID HOFFMAN, COFOUNDER OF LINKEDIN

So, why did I leave the relatively "safe" confines—not to mention the potentially huge rewards—of working at Lehman Brothers to dive into the world with my own business ventures? I did it because the whole "Big Corporate America" thing is simply not what I was born to do. It's also never that "safe."

You'll see what I mean as you continue reading.

While I greatly respect my friends and colleagues who've chosen the corporate route, my DNA simply wasn't made for embracing that path. How did I know? The people I meet and get to work with as an entrepreneur are one of the major reasons I left the corporate world to become an entrepreneur.

I don't know about you, but I genuinely love hanging with

other entrepreneurs. It excites me, but it also challenges me. (*Why didn't I think of that business concept?* or *Why couldn't I pull off that idea?*) I love the friendships I've created with fellow entrepreneurs, and I'm passionate about further understanding the mindset of like-minded people.

There are more reasons—enough to fill a book, which is kind of what I just did! Right now, however, I think it would be most helpful to share the general pieces of my overall experience. This is what enables me to offer genuine insider advice on the nuts and bolts of running a small business.

What on Earth Have I Done?

I couldn't begin a discussion of my past experiences without first giving credit to the start of it all: my entrepreneurial family—specifically, my father. He came into this world with that entrepreneurial spirit embedded in his core. Whether for good or bad, *it* was definitely passed on to me. I'm using the word "it" to mean entrepreneurship here. You either have *it*—or you don't. You can learn *it,* acquire *it,* be born with *it,* buy *it,* or marry into *it.* That doesn't matter. You do have to have *it.*

To kick my entrepreneurial spirit into gear at an early age, my parents raised me to value money. They also instilled in me the habit of making it on my own.

During elementary school, I started my first business. I called it JIS Car Washing. It wasn't a very creative name, considering I just used my initials—but it was a start.

It was 1982. I was very excited to have launched my first business, but I was even more excited about having my first business card. I'd started washing and waxing cars after school with the goal to raise enough money to buy a car by my senior year of high school.

It's always been much cooler having your own car in high school than having your parents drive you back and forth on dates. I was determined I wasn't going to wind up in that position. I could have tried to get the lead role in *The Karate Kid*, so that I'd get a car from Mr. Miyagi for my birthday (for those of you who remember the classic movie). Instead, I decided to start my first business. Those genes from my father were obviously already at work inside me.

If I remember correctly, I was earning a minimum of $200 per week—plus tips. The combination of working part-time, playing three varsity sports, and keeping up with homework made my days and weekends a busy blur, but I wouldn't have wanted it any other way.

Fortunately, my parents wavered a bit when it came time to actually purchase my first car. They agreed to put up 20 percent of the funds needed. Still, I had to earn the remaining 80 percent. It took an interesting, and yes difficult, balancing act to pull it off, but it didn't matter to me. I knew I wanted that car. Bad.

When I finally took the leap, I purchased a Nissan Maxima. For some reason, I thought it was more in vogue to have a car with a manual transmission, but more important, it was less expensive. The only problem: I couldn't stop at traffic lights on hills. I was afraid that I wouldn't get the car started again in first gear and would slip backward, crashing into the car behind me. But that was still okay with me. The stick shift was cool, so I made sure I had a car with a stick shift, hills or not.

On to College . . . and More Businesses

Following high school, I attended Tufts University, in Boston, Massachusetts. This is where I received my great liberal arts education. To augment my education, I also went to Boston University for specific business courses throughout the year.

I loved my college years—especially the semester I spent studying at the London School of Economics in London, England. (I probably didn't really need to say where the school was located, did I? The name itself provides a pretty strong hint as to its location.)

I graduated with a Bachelor of Arts degree in economics. (Tufts didn't offer a business degree, or I would have opted for that major.) However, during my junior and senior years of college, I started a company. In my junior year, I developed a line of T-shirts with the Tufts University mascot on them. The "Jumbo Bar Hopper" T-shirt became a popular item at school. I managed to convince a number of bars in Medford (a suburb of Boston) to sell them to students who frequented their establishments and sold nearly 3,000 shirts.

This turned out to be a great way to make some extra money while I was at school. It was also a fabulous way to meet girls—a perk very nearly as important to any college-age male as money. I also "hired" students to sell shirts to fellow students, local restaurants, and bars.

Don't ask me why the word "hired" is in quotes in that last paragraph. That's between those students and me. Let's just say there was bartering involved and leave it at that.

Into the Corporate Fray

Following four great years at Tufts, I consciously decided I wanted my first entrée into the business world to be a corporate experience. I knew my ultimate path would be that of an entrepreneur, but it was 1988. Investment banking was—and continues to be—a hot industry. I interviewed at many of the investment banks and, ultimately, chose to join Lehman Brothers. (More important, I was thankful they chose me.)

At Lehman, I earned my "degree" in working 100-plus hours per week. Believe me—this is only glamorous when you're talking about it. Getting home at midnight, even in a black Town Car, with my "free nightly dinner, as long as it costs less than the $15 meal allowance," loses its charm—in short order.

While I toiled away at my "day job" there, I continued thinking of ways I could become the master of my own destiny and start my own business. You could say a pattern was forming. It would shape my life forever.

Failure Is Part of the Process

"Don't worry about failure;
you only have to be right once."

—DREW HOUSTON, FOUNDER AND CEO OF DROPBOX

As you consider starting your own SB, there's one hard truth that pretty much smacks everyone in the face. I'm talking about the soul-searing fact that 50 percent of all small businesses fail within the first five years. I'll go more in depth into other important small business statistics shortly. For now, I want you to keep this 50 percent failure rate in mind. It's one of the major reasons why a lot of potentially successful entrepreneurs never try starting their own business.

It could be holding you back, too.

The point to remember is that it's hard starting your own business—and even harder to make it cash-positive. Then, it's harder still to create real value as you build, but it's also all far from impossible. And the risk of failure is far less than most people would have you believe. You also have roughly a 50 percent chance of success. That's a 50 percent chance of you personally succeeding in this gigantic, growing arena.

I would also argue that you'll enjoy a more satisfying life experience than your contemporaries in big business when you build your own successful small business, because you'll do it on your own—nobody will do it for you!

Which Risk Do You Prefer?

I'm amazed by how many people, even after understanding the real odds, still feel that starting a business is too much "risk" to assume. These same people will often put their entire lives into working for an employer, putting in their years with an eye constantly turned toward retirement—the "big prize" at the end of the corporate rainbow.

What do you suppose the odds are that their years of business-building for someone else will pay off with the long, blissful retirement they long for?

Hint: the odds aren't real high. Not at all. Certainly not more than 50 percent.

The lesson to take away here is that you can't fear failure and still successfully start or run a business of your own. The possibility of failure will always be present, regardless of which way you turn. The chances are about 50 percent that, whichever way you turn, it could be the wrong way. If you plan to be an entrepreneur, you need to get used to this. Embrace it, and you can make it work for you.

When it comes to making the decision between putting your whole life behind someone else's business and pouring everything you've got into one of your own, the odds aren't at all bet-ter either way. You might receive some pay along the way with an employer, but the rewards of working for someone else can't even begin to compete with the potential rewards of building and running a successful small business of your own.

It's important to keep this in mind as you consider a journey of your own into the entrepreneurial world: of course there's risk involved, but success in small business is far from impossible. I wouldn't be successful with my own businesses if it were. While it can be lonely and will be a lot of hard work along the way, you don't have to be alone in this endeavor.

Not with me here by your side.

Even thriving businesses experience many failures on their way to success. They also continue to experience them as they try to maintain their position in the market. You need to realize going in that you will fail—many times—along the way. The trick is to minimize the impact of those failures, so they can be overcome.

And, as I'm certain you've heard many times, you also must learn from your failures—even if you're sick of hearing this expression. I'm going to help you avoid a lot of the mistakes I made right here in this book, but I can't possibly clue you in to every possible failure you might hit along your own path. The unique lessons you learn by overcoming your own unique obsta-cles and failures can often make the difference in the success of your business.

Just know that failure is a part of the entrepreneurial process.

Far too few books on business provide this part of the pic-ture. They either gloss over it or overcomplicate it. It's vitally important to me that you have the whole picture.

The vast majority of companies ever launched don't enjoy

the immediate success you might think Uber, Twitter, or Lulu Lemon—to name just a few—achieved. Many brand names seemingly become ubiquitous in our lives overnight. In reality, most may have spent years launching and gaining market acceptance. The media—and you—noticed them as they finally took off.

It rarely happens "overnight," however you might define that word. Most SBs never see anything close to the levels of success that companies like these have seen, let alone getting to that level almost instantly.

Side Note: I have a concept for another book. Please don't copy it—if you can resist. I'd like to interview really, really smart CEOs and founders of start-ups and small businesses who failed. In short, this new book would be about companies that couldn't become profitable and had to shut their doors. It would also be interesting to follow those businesspeople who "failed" and study their future "successes." If you do decide to steal this idea, just make sure your book is poorly written so that I still have a shot with mine, okay? (I'm only half joking.)

Ideas do have value, and it's interesting how much one idea can mean to your future. But there are millions of ideas, and they're actually fairly easy to come by. Entrepreneurs see them everywhere. Opportunity lies waiting around every corner. How each of us executes those ideas—the unique twist and viewpoint we each can bring to the equation—makes all the difference. Add the right concerted action to bring that idea to fruition, however, and you could just have a business.

Whether that business is a success or not then relies entirely on you and the decisions you make moving forward from there. Usually, ideas come and go. Sometimes, however, the smallest things can trigger an idea that grows into a profitable enterprise.

Size Doesn't Matter

After Lehman: Golf Balls

It was actually a golf ball that gave me the idea for my first post–Lehman Brothers business. I'll tell you more about this business in just a bit. Meanwhile, don't tell anyone who was working at Lehman at the time, but I got things going with this new business while still clocking eighty of my usual one hundred hours a week for Lehman.

I'm kidding—especially if any of my past Lehman bosses are reading this book—for the most part. After getting home past 11 p.m., I would spend additional time, including the occasional rare free weekend when I wasn't working, preparing to launch my new venture.

It always takes time and dedication to actually get a business going. You've probably already had lots of "great" ideas for a new business—even before you thought about getting involved in starting one yourself. Taking action on one of those ideas, however, makes all the difference whether a successful business will actually be the result.

There's a lot more to this story, and I'll dive into it a little later on. However, before we go on, it's probably a good idea to also tell you what this book isn't going to be. If you've come into it with expectations I don't plan to meet, I want you to feel free to stop reading right now.

In *Size Doesn't Matter*, topics covered will NOT include:

○ Help with writing a business plan

○ Instructions on how to use Facebook, Twitter, and other social media for marketing

○ The best type of legal structure for your business

○ Tips on crowdfunding to raise start-up capital

○ Expert advice on bank financing or venture capital

It's okay with me if you're now ready to put the book in your friend's mailbox as a birthday gift because you were hoping some of the above topics would be covered. (At least you bought the book!) However, I recommend you read at least one more chapter before you pass it along. I have a lot more info and insights to share with you, and you might just decide it's worthwhile to hang around a bit longer.

4:00 A.M.

Facts Don't Lie . . .

> "There's nothing wrong with staying small.
> You can do big things with a small team."
> —JASON FRIED, FOUNDER OF 37SIGNALS

I'd like to dispel the notion that owning and operating an SB is somehow less than ideal—or that your business isn't "successful" if it's classified as small. The truth is, there are far more small or very small businesses serving their founders perfectly well without ever growing into giant corporations with hundreds of employees.

Still, for whatever reason, I find that many employees of Fortune 500 and Fortune 1000 companies tend to look down on businesspeople who run small businesses. They tend to look upon "small business" as if we're all some kind of lesser entities.

That attitude is dead wrong. Collectively, small business is anything but small.

You should understand before we proceed that I love the idea of small business and everything that goes with it. I love SBs so much that I can't stop myself from starting them and working with them over and over again.

I haven't been medically diagnosed with attention deficit disorder (ADD), but I do suspect I have *business* attention deficit disorder. I just now thought of that catchy term. The acronym BADD is even catchier. I may try to copyright that!

I'm BADD to the bone.

I've got the business bug BADD.

This could be a new business idea. It's clearly how ideas for them are born, and you just witnessed it firsthand right on this page. Just imagine . . . T-shirts, cups, office accessories—all emblazoned with the "BADD" logo.

Anyway, I do believe I suffer from BADD. I tend to thrive on starting and running businesses. Note: I said, "businesses." That's because, whether they fail or succeed, I find myself doing it again and again.

But I swear I'm not crazy, and I never tend to ignore the odds, even though there is risk involved. Sometimes, you have to be willing to risk everything. But, unlike betting it all on red in Vegas, the risk in business is manageable within certain limits. You have some control over the odds, and they're always better than any casino would be willing to offer you.

There are plenty of statistics proving that the Fortune 500 attitude about small business ownership is wrong.

Starting your business is difficult, but so is working in a high-level position in corporate America. It's also actually no more risky than trying to land a job in a major corporation or trying to hold on to that position for years, hoping to eventually work your way to the top. These folks face the perils of corporate bureaucracy, earnings reports, and senior management who, many times, are risk-averse and far too content with the status quo.

For now, I want to emphasize that, regardless of where you currently work or wherever your business path takes you (or, hopefully, you take it), it's impossible to ignore the huge impact small business has on our economy today.

Small Business Isn't Just Big: It's GIGANTIC!

The next time you're confronted by someone who half snickers when you say you run an SB, just recite a few of these facts (as provided by the Small Business Administration):

○ There are roughly twenty-three million small businesses in the United States. Together, they account for 54 percent of all sales in the country.

○ All told, small businesses provide 55 percent of all jobs—and they've provided 66 percent of all net new jobs since the 1970s.

○ More than 600,000 of those small businesses are franchises. In the United States, they account for 40 percent of all retail sales and provide jobs for eight million people.

○ Landlords should love small businesses, too. The small business sector in the United States currently occupies 30 to 50 percent of all commercial space—an estimated twenty to thirty-four billion square feet.

While our friends in corporate America have been downsizing, the number of small business start-ups has grown and continues to grow rapidly. As a result, the total number of small businesses in the United States has increased by 49 percent—just since 1982.

There's even better news. Remember that failure rate? You know, the one I recommended you focus on earlier, the one that brings so many entrepreneurial hopefuls to a screeching halt before ever getting a business off the ground? It's still high, at 50 percent, but it has steadily declined over the years.

Half Full or Half Empty?

I understand. Really I do. A 50 percent failure rate still sounds rough to the otherwise faint of heart—until you remember this also means that 50 percent don't fail. To put it more succinctly, 50 percent also succeed.

Unless you start your own casino, those are much better odds than you'd ever see in Vegas. They're definitely better than most any legitimate investment vehicle would provide.

If the risk still freezes you when you think of starting an SB of your own, you need to realize that working as an employee is no "sure deal" either. In fact, since 1990, statistics show that big business eliminated four million jobs while small businesses created eight million new jobs.

Many Entrepreneurs—Lots of Hats

While I'm tossing out statistics like a college professor, I'll add some more to the mix. A 2011 study by the Small Business and Entrepreneurship Council used U.S. Census Bureau data, showing that there were 5.68 million "employer" firms in the United States, as its basis. The study found that some 99.7 percent of "employer" firms employed fewer than 500 employees each. Of this group, 89.8 percent employed fewer than twenty workers each, and 22.7 percent were classified as "non-employer"—meaning that the owner does everything and hires no employees for help.

Add all those numbers together and we find that, thanks to the insights provided by this study, the number of firms with fewer than 500 employees increased by 99.9 percent, while companies with fewer than twenty workers increased by 98 percent!

It's pretty amazing when you see the numbers laid out like this. I don't know about you, but these statistics make me more excited about being an entrepreneur. I feel entrepreneurship enables me to play a part in what is obviously a small business explosion—a revolution in business that's coming about because of entrepreneurs like you and me.

"Big" Is Losing Its Allure

Based on industry figures, the chances are good you'll work for someone else—whether in a small or large company. I've said working for someone else is not at all the "security blanket" you were taught it was in school years ago, but this is obviously still where most people wind up.

In fact, things in the SB arena are heating up so much that the allure of corporate America is actually on the wane. Being an entrepreneur has now actually become "cool" compared to joining corporations that comprise the Nasdaq or Standard & Poor's 500. The concept of being a "lifer," earning the twenty-five-year pin by spending your entire career at one large company—eventually rising in the ranks from analyst, to associate, to director, to vice president, to senior vice president, to managing director, and, finally, to partner—is no longer in vogue. Not with my friends, anyway.

My contemporaries have lost their patience. They don't want to wait a few decades to have that great title and finally earn their payday. If it's going to take decades, many would now prefer working those decades in a business they've created themselves, enjoying the daily excitement, energy, and unlimited potential returns for their effort.

How Long Will It Grow?

With all the rosy statistics coming out of the small and very small business sector these days, it's easy to wonder how long the current growth will continue. I usually answer this by comparing the 1988 market (when I graduated from Tufts) to where it's at today.

When I graduated, most of my class was interviewing at Xerox, IBM, General Electric, and huge multinational banks. The hope was to start climbing the corporate ladder to a nice corner office. This is no longer the case. These Fortune 500 companies are no longer in vogue the way they were in those days. In some cases, they're no longer even in business!

The most popular large companies to join today? Apple, Google, Uber, and similar rising tech giants that, except for Apple, didn't even exist twenty-five years ago. In the case of Apple, it was just a small start-up in a California garage back then.

If you do the research, you'll find that graduates are now looking longingly for work at a wealth of companies that mostly all started out very small not that long ago with little expectation of becoming what they are today.

This should actually be encouraging as you look into the possibility of starting your own business. You need to know the failure rate. Still, it never hurts to dream, and it's certainly nice to know that most of the huge, successful businesses today started out small—just like the business you're thinking about starting.

Welcome to the New Corner Office . . . in Your Basement

By starting your own business or joining a start-up venture, you get to choose your title immediately, even if you have no employees working for you and your corner office is in your basement. Whatever—it still sounds cool when you introduce yourself as president of a company at cocktail parties!

So, there's no guarantee that the long-awaited payday from working inside corporate America will come. Stock prices change. Big companies are sold, merged, not sold, and not acquired. Shit happens. Promotions are guaranteed, then yanked away in seconds when your manager gets fired with no notice. Young people take over for more senior and tenured personnel. Traveling on no notice, getting stuck in airports, and missing family events in the process gets really old. You're simply not the master of your life, and the ultimate payoff is pretty much out of your control.

Most people working in corporate American really don't control their destiny. Some do get lucky. The state lottery has winners, too, after all. Still, I'm sure you hate it as much as I do when your not-so-smart friend who barely got into college joins a large multinational company and, by pure good fortune, luck, and perseverance, there's an IPO, and he or she makes millions. You may not readily admit it (unless you go to church confession or repent for your sins on the Jewish holidays), but I know you hate it.

We all know friends who married into successful family businesses. Good for them! Does it make you jealous? Maybe they really aren't that happily married. There's also probably a very strict prenuptial agreement, so it's not all that it seems to be. It can also all be yanked away at any time, before you ever reach it, often due to circumstances beyond your control.

Delusions of Smallness

So, small is growing—so much so that it's becoming cool. Now that the corporate tide has turned, so to speak, you'll catch people who aren't entrepreneurs trying to claim they are.

I'm always amused when my corporate friends try to argue that they're really entrepreneurs, even though they operate within the framework of a big company. The company might say they want to foster an "entrepreneurial spirit" among their employees. But these people are only kidding themselves.

Whenever I hear them, I quickly say to myself, *Yeah, right—sure they're entrepreneurs! They're completely on their own as they gaze over Midtown Manhattan from their comfortable high-rise offices, provided and paid for by their benevolent employers.*

They might be "in the trenches." They could, possibly, be guiding a new large company through the mine-filled harbors to growth. But they have full support staffs helping them every step of the way, too—also paid for by the company. They don't have to think twice about the cost of sending a letter to a prospective client by FedEx—the company's paying the bill.

I seriously doubt they ever go to bed wondering about making payroll. I also doubt they've ever jumped out of a fretful sleep at 4:00 a.m. to ensure that a subjective holiday bonus is paid—even though the word "subjective" has lost all meaning. It's been paid the past ten years, and the employees now expect that payment to buy holiday gifts and pay for their annual vacations, so you have to make sure it's done. I also doubt they've ever dealt with a frivolous lawsuit that's impacting employee morale or with the broken Internet line that's basically closed the company until it's working again. In corporate America, they have separate departments to handle all these issues—and more—for them within minutes.

Do I sound envious? You can bet I am! But I still wouldn't want to trade places.

Granted, people who achieve great success in corporate America might have to jump through plenty of hoops and work hard to get the job. They've also dealt with the politics and ass-kissing required to keep their employment as they move up the rungs of the corporate ladder. Whatever your impressions of entrepreneurs might be, I'd still argue that there's little comparison, and it is a noble, brave endeavor. It's also a lot more difficult to start, grow, and develop a new business than it is to join a well-established company as an executive-level employee.

Pardon My Lack of Corporate Enthusiasm

You've probably noticed I tend to wax a bit sarcastic with many of my big company comments. I hope you realize there's a healthy dose of good-natured jabbing going on there. I realize many people in corporate America are incredibly smart, have numerous master's degrees, and work years to achieve their levels of professional success. Remember—I traveled that path, too . . . for a while.

But this is a book about the entrepreneur and small business owner, written for entrepreneurs and small business owners by one of their own. We're entitled to have a bit of fun at corporate America's expense—at least until a major book publisher with a fat enough upfront signing bonus contacts me to write a book about the benefits of Corporate America. I might quickly change my position then . . . just kidding!

I'm hoping we can keep the exchange we're enjoying right here going. Just continue reading—and don't forget there are some blank pages in the back of the book for any thoughts that may come into your brain as your read. Please write something down there now. It'll make me feel more like we're having an interactive conversation as you read.

Meanwhile, before we dive in further, I just thought of some business successes and challenges that would be good to share in the next chapter. These stories are, in one way or the other, at least partially responsible for the unique wisdom I believe I bring to the table on this topic.

5:00 A.M.

Testing All the Waters

> "The value of an idea lies in the using of it."
> —THOMAS EDISON, BUSINESSMAN AND INVENTOR

As I mentioned earlier, I launched my first business in grammar school with my car washing and waxing business. I then continued, in college, with my Jumbo Bar Hopper T-shirt business.

It was during my senior year, however, that I had the idea to start Sports Impressions. This is the business I mentioned earlier, the one that was inspired by golf balls. Although Sports Impressions never turned into a commercial success, I still think it was one of my most clever and intriguing concepts to date.

During college, I wanted to learn to play golf (because so many business people told me it's a great skill to have for meeting people—plus, it's fun to have some beers with friends on weekends while swinging the club, hopefully less than a hundred times). This is why my friends and I started visiting the driving ranges, as an outlet from studying. While there, I continued to look down at this white circular golf ball that had "Range" imprinted on it.

That's when I had a huge "aha" moment.

I thought, *Why can't an advertiser's name appear on that ball at the thousands of golf ranges across the USA? After all, golfers will constantly stare at it during the average half-hour or one-hour range visit.*

With that idea and just a few hundred dollars, I started Sports Impressions. This is how I began my quest to have corporate-branded golf balls at driving ranges throughout the United States.

I was successful in securing test orders from the local Coca-Cola bottler and from a regional real estate brokerage firm. I was ecstatic! I then started working out the logistics with Top Flite, a golf ball manufacturer, to produce the balls. Then, I cut deals with the local range owners to make my clients' balls available.

Please don't say that too loudly in public. It wouldn't sound right out of context.

The business itself seemed pretty simple. I was about to make real money. How could this not work? I'd obviously discovered the next great idea!

A Flaw in the Ointment

Once an initial test was concluded at a local golf range, I targeted the next fifty ranges as prospects in the Northeast. Then, I was going to hire a national staff to quickly roll the concept out nationwide. But there were some significant flaws in my model—too numerous to mention in this book. One "biggie" that became a major obstacle, however, was the constant pounding the corporate advertisers' logo took on those balls. It quickly turned their beautiful logos into a horrific mess, looking more like a coloring book scribble on a broken golf ball.

Failing Up?

Following my graduation from college, as I mentioned earlier, I joined Lehman Brothers in the investment banking division. This provided me with great long-term financial experience, even though I knew it wasn't my calling. During my tenure at Lehman Brothers, I did get the opportunity to be involved in the sale of Rockefeller Center in New York City. This was one of the largest real estate transactions in history at the time. Kind of noteworthy in those circles.

To illustrate my value to the team, however, I was presented with a $200 Mont Blanc pen (which I unfortunately lost within a few weeks of the closing). Meanwhile, my boss earned millions of dollars in bonus money. So much for the great rewards of corporate life.

Something great did come out of my time there. While I was still working ridiculous hours at Lehman, I met my girlfriend—and now my wife—Jill Gilson.

Side Note: I figured I had to mention her in this book. After all, overlooking it would be analogous to not mentioning your wife when winning a Grammy Award, right?

Of course, I asked Jill to marry me because I genuinely loved her. Still, I also have to admit I loved the fact that she worked for the National Basketball Association. How many young guys who love sports end up dating a gorgeous girl who works in sports and loves them, too? She "had me at hello" (as coined in the Jerry McGuire movie)—especially when she handed me her NBA business card on our blind date.

Twenty-five years after meeting her, we're still more than happily married, with three wonderful children—even though she no longer works for the NBA.

Worth a Closer Look

Through Jill's contacts at the NBA, she introduced me to a Chinese gentleman who had created white paper binoculars. This was one of his various SKUs in his product line out of thousands of promotional products. While working late one evening at the bank, I came up with the idea to put company logos on his product. Wow! Paper binoculars that really worked, all ready for printing with company logos.

Remember what I said about the entrepreneurial mind never stopping, always turning? This was one of those times that the brain-that-never-shuts-up of mine delivered a real payoff.

You probably noticed I like logos. What can I say? I'm a huge fan of marketing and love selling to other businesses. That makes marketing and marketing specialty items natural for me.

As a result, Spectoculars was founded. I started prospecting for clients for my new promotional product. After many sales calls with different leagues and corporate advertisers, I was able to secure an order for 250,000 units for the NFL Super Bowl on behalf of my advertiser, Breathe Right Nasal Strips. That one event led to more sales—to HBO, CNN Sports, and Coca-Cola.

Give 'Em What They Really Want

A business was born. Other companies started requesting different types of promotional items—branded T-shirts, hats, umbrellas, and a variety of other products. I had no idea how to make or secure these products, but why turn away a sale? Like any good entrepreneur, I said, "Thank you for the order," and then figured out how to deliver! This resulted in the formation of Mericom Marketing, Inc., a promotional marketing firm.

Are you asking yourself how I thought of this name? Good question. Most of the names I wanted were already taken, so it was a combination of three words: America, merit, and communications.

Boom!

What began as a simple one-person company eventually turned into a company of nineteen people, based in New Jersey, with an office in London and a sourcing office in Hong Kong. Doesn't it sound big, having offices around the world? In all candor, my London office was a fax machine, sitting in my friend's bedroom. Hong Kong was "sort of" an office. We had a sourcing agent representing us on large orders that needed to be fulfilled and shipped from overseas to the States.

Anyway, we also started fulfilling traditional promotional product requests. Eventually, we hired designers to create proprietary products for our corporate clients. As the company grew, we started a Company Store Division. This new division stocked various merchandise for our clients in-house. This enabled us to offer same-day delivery for traditional branded product choices.

Side Note: I love using the word "division," and use it anytime

I can. Even if the business is just me. It gives the impression of being a significantly larger company.

After running Mericom for eight years, I think my BADD took over. I started getting bored. I was also frustrated by the industry for a variety of reasons. This is when I started seeking out my next business challenge.

Throughout my business career, one recurring theme is: business is business. Yes, there might be some different terminology involved, depending on your industry, but the core principles remain the same. You should always look for opportunities within your industry where you can leverage your existing customer base and the relationships you've built into additional business. It's imperative! But don't forget to look outside your business and your industry at new and emerging industries that might also present opportunity. This is where my attention was wandering during my unrest as Mericom grew.

It's never easy coming up with something entirely new. Never underestimate the enormity of this task. Keep this in mind as you keep an eye on potential existing opportunities in the world outside the box.

The Perfect Segue to My Most Recent Fourteen Years in Business

Following my exit from the promotional products industry, I was introduced—through a family friend who was involved in the banking industry—to the credit card processing and payments industry. I'm very fortunate he did and equally fortunate that he subsequently became my business partner.

We All Use 'Em—Why Not Turn 'Em into a Business?

Yes, we all use our credit cards to purchase items at retailers, food at restaurants, and different products and services from the Internet. Most people, however, don't understand the behind-the-scenes process of how a merchant (the technical term for a "business" in our industry) gets set up to accept the four major card types—Visa, MasterCard, American Express, and Discover. Fewer still understand the other payment services related to payment processing, including check acceptance, gift cards, and stored value cards, to name a few of the most prevalent.

Fast-forward: we founded Charge Card Systems, Inc., a national credit card processing service that helps a myriad of companies with their credit card processing requirements. With lots of hard work and a little luck, we grew the company relatively quickly. In addition to our full-time in-house personnel, we had approximately 600 independent agents selling our payment processing nationwide. This was when I noticed, as it was for most businesses, 80 percent of our revenue was derived from the top 20 percent of our sales personnel. This is the well-known 80/20 rule, and it's most certainly in action in our business (probably closer, in my situation, to the 90/10 rule).

We loved the business and, in 2012, sold it to Card Connect. This was a national payments firm rolling up payments companies under one umbrella. The acquisition of our company was their largest to date, and I stayed on as president of Charge Card Systems during the transition period.

In addition to managing Charge Card Systems, we founded two other companies in the payments sphere that weren't part of the acquisition: Alternative Merchant Processing, Inc., which is devoted to working with high-risk merchants who don't fit the traditional merchant processing underwriting model, and Charge Card Funding, LLC, which is focused on providing working capital to merchants on a nationwide scale.

Both of these companies are still operational and growing.

6:00 A.M.

A Small Business Serving Small Business? Priceless!

> "Don't try to be original, just try to be good."
> —PAUL RAND, ART DIRECTOR AND GRAPHIC ARTIST
> (INCLUDING LOGOS FOR IBM, UPS, ABC)

As I recollect my business experiences to date, one overriding theme becomes evident: with the exception of the time I spent working at Lehman, my work has always served the needs of other small businesses. Because of this, I've also gained invaluable insight into the workings of literally thousands of other small businesses. This has enabled me to learn more every day through my interaction with them as clients, vendors, prospects, and friends.

I could easily fill another 900 pages with all the stories and experiences, but . . . enough is enough for now. We should move along. It's probably time to brush the theories and "maybes" aside so we can get down to the meat-and-potatoes of how all this small business stuff really works.

Drilling Down to Real

Earlier, I spilled out a bunch of statistics. They highlighted exactly how ripe the atmosphere is today for starting or joining a small or very small business—more so than at any other time in history. So, half of all small or very small companies will fail in their first five years. This means that half of new small businesses also make it for at least five years. Let's keep this going. Among those surviving businesses—about a quarter go on to make it to the all-mighty fifteen-year mark.

It's all a matter of numbers. And you control much of what determines how far your business will go. One of the best things you can do, then, is focus on increasing your odds of success with your business. It would be great if there were a way to determine with certainty whether a new business would pay off for you or not. Unfortunately, it's not quite that simple.

There are, unfortunately, a thousand or more variables that determine whether your company will achieve success. That's why there are countless reasons some companies in competitive markets thrive while others wither and die. It's often frustrating trying to nail it down—kind of like hammering nails into Jell-O.

Increase Your Odds of Success— Satisfy a Preexisting Need

There is a way to increase your odds of success dramatically. Locate a market already served by successful businesses, then find a way to serve that market even better. I learned this concept just recently—find a problem that already exists in the market you want to enter and just fix it. If you do, "they will come!"

There's another signal you can watch for. It will indicate you've found the right business or industry. You'll see this signal when you look into a business that feels like you are genuinely fulfilling a customer's needs.

In 2010, I experienced the power of these two concepts firsthand as a customer when I had a very small accounting firm helping me with my annual taxes. The firm was a two-person company: a CPA, who was a super guy in his seventies with tons of experience with individuals and closely held companies, and his assistant. The CPA was gregarious, smart, and great at tax planning. Unfortunately, he didn't use email or texting to communicate. This was a problem for me. I didn't want to always have to make a phone call to handle a quick issue.

Bottom line: as much as I liked him personally and, as good as the quality of his work was, I had to switch. I needed a more progressive and technologically advanced accounting firm (as if email and texting are advanced technologies today).

I don't think I was being at all unreasonable in this case. It wouldn't matter if I was. I took my business elsewhere. I now work with another small accounting firm with around eight professionals and support personnel. My communication with them is perfect, using all the tools I prefer using—including telephone calls—when necessary.

This accounting firm is doing great work, and they've capitalized on meeting the needs of a "younger generation" and millennials that are accustomed to more progressive modes of communication. Simple.

Exterminating the Exterminator

In 2003, I used an exterminating company that had an archaic back-office system. Invoices would come sporadically throughout the year, requesting payments be made by check. There were also disputes throughout the year, because the firm wasn't organized in its accounting. It was becoming a major problem for me just keeping track of whether I'd paid him, if he'd received my check, and to which open invoice it was being applied. I was essentially forced to do the company's accounting for them when it came to my billing and service.

This was my pain point. I decided to see if I could eliminate the pain.

My neighbor had been working with an exterminating firm that accepted credit cards and kept the credit card on file to automatically pay for quarterly service. Bottom line: this company served my pain point and issue. Again, as much as I personally liked the former company and its founder, and the actual service was fine, I needed to switch to a more progressive company. The new company had found a unique differentiator—especially in 2003, when mobile payments weren't as popular as they are today with the advent of Square and other mobile payment solutions that are now available to anyone starting a business.

As you consider which business you're interested in going into, here are some ideas: According to a recent article in Forbes, the fastest-growing businesses in 2011 were auto-repair shops, beauty salons, and dry cleaners. Does that mean they are in 2015? Maybe not. But, as of this writing, the statistics will be available soon. The point here is that it's important to do your homework to increase your odds of launching a successful business. The information is available. See what's likely to be successful before committing yourself to starting a business.

You also have to be able to find unique ways to outsmart your competition if you want to launch a business that not only survives, but also thrives. Research and planning are essential here as well.

You've most likely found that careful planning is extremely important before you jump into anything new. Starting a business is no different. It's also one of the most important things you'll ever do. It's right up there with getting married. Before you leap, the planning and research you do will help you determine what you need to know about the industry you plan to enter—and to study the people buying from that industry.

Yes, it feels like homework. It is homework, if you must know. And it seems like it goes on forever. It doesn't—and you always learn something new as you move through the planning process.

Get Started or Go Home

I do have one caution for you here—and it might sound like I'm contradicting myself slightly when you hear it: at some point, you just need to get started! Make a sales call, and start the process. Without a client, you're not in business. Despite my stressing over the importance of planning, I've seen too many entrepreneurs think and rethink their concept to the point that they never truly begin.

What a shame! Who knows how many of their ideas were really good? Maybe one or two would have changed the whole world! We could all be poorer for them never coming into being.

My own story is an excellent case to study. I knew nothing

about the credit card industry when I got involved in the payments industry—except for a few important facts. My research turned up the following nuggets that excited me about the possibilities:

1. It was an industry where merchants ordinarily didn't have much of a relationship with their credit card processing partners, if at all. Basically, they had no relationship. Most of the other industry players didn't even know their clients' names.

2. The industry was enormous, with millions of potential merchant clients.

3. There were no accounts receivables as payments.

4. I could develop a scalable business.

5. It generated recurring revenue, commonly called residual income.

I was sold.

The light bulb went off. I could see that this could be a good business for me. I'd discovered a pain point in a large potential industry with plenty of existing users.

When my friends heard this story, some said, "You're crazy going into such a competitive business." I looked it at completely differently. I said, "It's not competitive, because nobody knows who their processor is. All I need to do is offer a good solution, plus great customer service, and develop a solid relationship with the merchants. How hard can that be?"

Within a decade, we had worked with over 13,000 merchants and had developed a successful, thriving business.

When Alone Isn't Really Alone

Another important point you need to consider as you begin planning: you need to decide whether the small business you're starting will operate with or without employees. This one decision plays heavily in my definition of whether a business is a small business or a very small business.

If you do decide to proceed without employees—at least at the start—you certainly won't be alone. Seventy-five percent of all businesses in the United States are non-employer businesses. Even better, you can take heart in the fact that total revenues from non-employer businesses reached $989.9 billion in 2011—a 4.1 percent increase from 2010. And those revenues continue to climb.

But again, I'm wandering—I should probably get back to my story.

The business did very well, when all is said and done. We were able to sell it to a much larger company and "cash out"—a common success goal for many entrepreneurs.

Still, you might be surprised to learn that not everybody wants to build a business they can ultimately sell. Some owners want to develop a legacy business that can be passed down to future generations. Others want to use their business as a means to travel around the world to great places. I think you get the point. Believe it or not, money is not the driving factor or the end goal for every business.

The cool thing is that it's your decision what you choose to do with your own business when you start one! You decide everything.

Why Do Otherwise Sane Men and Women Ever Take This Path Less Traveled?

> "There's lots of bad reasons to start a company. But there's only one good, legitimate reason, and I think you know what it is: it's to change the world."
>
> —PHIL LIBIN, CEO OF EVERNOTE

The reasons why someone would choose the path of entrepreneurship are many and varied. They might simply like how it feels to blaze a new trail out of the business wilderness, digging the rocks out of the field as they go. Maybe they want to remove the ceiling from their lifetime earnings potential. They might feel they'd be better at what they do for a living if they're calling the shots, no longer limited by the restraints placed upon them by an employer.

Why are you considering taking the leap?

There are also, to be honest, solid reasons why someone might make the decision to work for someone else. I firmly believe everyone should at least consider the possibility of starting their own business before making this decision, but that's certainly up to each individual. Still, some people feel they simply aren't cut out for the entrepreneurial life. Even knowing that working for someone else is no guarantee of anything, they still like the feeling that it's more certain and the steady pay along the way. Perhaps they simply prefer letting someone else worry about running the show.

Go figure—right?

Either way, it's definitely a personal decision—one you'll generally wind up making with your gut. One thing's certain: everyone who enters the world of entrepreneurship, whether joining the leadership in a small business or starting a business from scratch, becomes a member of a truly unique club.

Welcome to the Club!

Once you do make this decision, you'll find you share a lot of similar thoughts, ideas, experiences, and feelings other entrepreneurs have—whether they run businesses in your industry or not.

That's why I consider it a club. A very special—but far from exclusive—club. I especially like the fact that it's a club that's open to everyone. You've probably noticed in my own story . . . even grade school and college kids are welcome to join. The club isn't closed to anyone, and that's what makes it truly exciting.

Despite all the possible reasons why people start businesses and the vast differences in the types of people who do, everyone in this entrepreneurial "club" shares a number of characteristics:

- We all want more control in our lives.
- We realize there are also risks when you work for someone else, someone who directs things for you—hopefully in a way that takes you where you wanted to go.
- We don't want a ceiling on our earnings potential.
- We don't mind working long, hard hours to get the rewards a business of our own can bring us.

Spend some serious time thinking this through. If you're not cut out for the challenge of starting or joining a small business, it's best that you back off the notion right here and now. For this reason, I want to focus a bit more on the various traits and skills you'll need to call upon to make the most of this journey you're considering. Some of what you hear from me might sound discouraging. If you feel discouraged, run—don't walk—to the time clock nearest you.

That might come at you kind of like a rude slap in the face. You'll thank me later: I could be saving you the loss of your life savings. There's no shame in working for someone else. Some people truly believe they have the entrepreneurial spirit to work on their own, and some were born to join a well-established larger company with all the perks and benefits that come with it.

There are certainly plenty of companies you can work for that provide a work environment similar to the entrepreneurial experience. Whether you're the CEO-type or you wish to join an existing company as senior management or you simply want the template given to you (as with the franchisor/franchisee model), there are positions you can find that could work well for you. Unless, of course, you're infected with the entrepreneurial bug.

The Feeling I Didn't Get

I proved to myself that I can play the corporate game. I achieved success by moving up the corporate ladder while I was an analyst at Lehman Brothers. I now understand the mentality of corporate America, even all the bureaucracy and human resource issues, thanks to that experience.

Similar to starting my own companies, working at Lehman Brothers required that I put in an incredible amount of work and very long hours. For me, it wasn't ever rewarding enough. I wasn't passionate about the job. Putting that many hours into something that doesn't generate a true sense of excitement for me stops being interesting—in a big hurry.

As the most junior member of my team, there was an unwritten, yet spoken rule that junior people never leave the office prior to the more senior personnel—in case they might need our services. I did try to sneak out several times, but I always got caught! I felt like I was in business jail!

It could work out totally differently for you. Hats off if that environment is where you shine. I didn't, but in all candor, I have many friends who stuck it out and now, years later, have achieved great financial and professional success.

When my team at Lehman actually sold the iconic Rockefeller Center, however, even that gigantic champagne-popping sale failed to give me the sense of satisfaction I was looking for. In fact, it was the feeling I didn't get from being a part of this enormous sale that played directly into my decision to work hard, instead, at being an entrepreneur.

My managers at Lehman Brothers respected me and liked my work and work ethic. I could easily have stayed on in my analyst position and eventually gone on to associate and grow within the organization from there. The financial rewards common with the life of the investment banking industry could have been mine. Still, I never fit into the corporate model. Accomplishing things for myself gives me a greater sense of pleasure, because I'm then free to choose to do something special.

There's no right or wrong answer when it comes to making my own decisions—the right choice is what's right for me and that will also apply to you.

When in Doubt—Test!

While you consider your options, I think it's very helpful for you to take a work assessment test for yourself. One of the best-known tests is Wonderlic. There are also many other tests you can take online. These tests will enable you to better assess your own skill sets, discover what you enjoy doing most, see what you're best at doing, and a whole lot more. They can help provide candid and honest information on your skill sets.

You need this kind of information if you're at all still in doubt about whether or not you're cut out to be an entrepreneur. For example, from these exams, I know that I'm a strategic thinker, a people person, and a sales guy. I also know I don't have the aptitude and skill set for such tedious functions as accounting, engineering, or architecture—no offense intended to anyone who does. Knowing what I'm good at, I can make the best use of my skills. Knowing what I'm not good at enables me to avoid putting myself in position for failure.

Often, corporate management doesn't use the testing tools now easily available to determine the best fit for an employee within the organization. This is a common mistake I see being made with all types of companies, big or small. It's one reason, I believe, that many people like me leave the corporate arena. Maybe John Smith can't do job "A," but would be a superstar in job "B." They should be using these tests.

Side Note: I'm not sure why I always use this commonplace name for examples—I'm sorry if your name is actually John Smith.

You should look up the tests online. Take them to help you decide if you're really entrepreneurial material. They'll also help you better position yourself, whichever decision you make.

What Do You Really Love?

People often ask me why I chose to be an entrepreneur. I already touched on this in an earlier chapter . . . as it applies to most people. My answer has changed throughout the years, as I have changed. But it's also always been short.

It used to be, "I want to become a millionaire and make lots of money." Now that I'm closing in on fifty, however, my answer is that I want my freedom. I want to do it all my way. I also want to be a great dad and husband who spends lots of quality time with his family.

Don't get me wrong . . . these things do require money. The more, the better. However—and I mean this sincerely—my life would not be terribly different from how I live today if I had that $50 million I used to dream about acquiring when I was first starting out.

Side Note: There is one exception to this: if I did have $50 million, I'd have to fly in a private jet and avoid ever taking a coach flight again. I've suffered enough at the hands of coach throughout the years.

When people ask if I love what I do for a living, my quick answer is, "I like it a lot. But I love hanging out with my family, attending activities with my kids, and playing golf."

It's always a balance. Launching or operating an SB can be all-consuming, but you can't be so blinded by what you're trying to do in your business that you forget the things that really matter in life. This probably sounds difficult. It probably sounds slightly contrary to the overall entrepreneurial theme as you thought of it coming into this book.

As for the business itself—for me—it's the people who make the work fun. I adore meeting with other small business owners from all over the United States and around the world. Hearing their stories and sharing tips and ideas with them fascinates me. On top of that, my business affords me the opportunity to earn great income and financial rewards for my family.

8:00 A.M.

It's Never Just about the Money

> "A business that makes nothing but money
> is a poor business."
>
> —HENRY FORD, FOUNDER OF FORD MOTOR COMPANY

In my formative business years, I dreamed of making lots of money. That may still be your goal. There's nothing wrong with wanting financial security and all the trappings that come with it. However, as I said already, what I find I'm really looking for now is the freedom to live my life, to attend my children's events at school, and to spend time with my wife (and, yes, having the money to pay for everything makes it all much nicer). Running my own businesses provides me that freedom.

Ride Your Cycle to Success . . . for You

We also all have cycles to our personal and professional lives—times when doing one thing fits better, and at other times, something else fits better. That's why there's no one roadmap to business success. If someone tries to tell you there is, run. Get away quickly. They're lying.

Your personal definition of success and how you choose to achieve it—at this time in your life—is the one that should guide this decision.

Consider this example: My cousin Bruce has lived in Aspen, Colorado, for the past forty-plus years, where he taught mountain climbing to locals and northeastern yuppies trying to show off to their girlfriends and wives how athletic they are as they propelled down the mountain. In his thirties, he was a world-renowned mountain and ice climber, having reached the top of the fifth highest summit in the Himalayas, 27,766 feet above sea level—and he did it without oxygen. He now flies a single-engine, small-propeller plane for a nonprofit organization to educate people interested in the wilderness about the conservation problem facing America and the world.

Bruce is living every guy's dream. He's his own person, loves the outdoors, and wouldn't have it any other way. You might say it's idyllic.

Do you think Bruce would have ever enjoyed—or thrived—working in a 10'-x-10' interior office with no windows in Midtown Manhattan, surviving the bureaucracy of corporate America? Of course not! Now, he's enjoyed his life, hiking for days in the mountains and surviving bear sightings. He's essentially living his dream—a vision made even dreamier by the fact that it's also provided him with a living.

But these are his priorities; mine are far from risking my life on a mountaintop. I'm much more turned on by risking my capital to grow a business. Your priorities will likely vary, and as well they should. What makes each of us happy is going to be different. We all choose our path—you and I may get to the finish line differently, but as entrepreneurs, it's our race, and I do know the life I've chosen is a way to make some unbelievable dreams come true.

I'm happy with that choice.

Your Values Matter

Consider your own values. They're a significant factor when you're thinking about launching a business. This includes the things your family needs besides money.

The trite expression about life being all about your family and your health really is true. When I talk about the determination and willpower required to make a business work, that includes doing everything the business requires and maintaining your connection with your family.

Remember when I said I wanted a car for my senior year of high school and worked hard to make the money—while maintaining my grades and participation in sports? You have to want to own your own business that bad. Is it more fun to be able to afford new shoes, dine out for expensive dinners, and vacation often? Of course! But it's not a great goal by itself. We all know many "wealthy" people who aren't happy and don't live what we would honestly consider a "rich" life, regardless of the money and success they might have. I know people like this. I'm sure you do as well.

Without resorting to labels or stereotypes, I wouldn't be truly candid if I didn't share that my family is enjoying an above-average lifestyle. Within reasonable limits, we don't have to go without whatever it is we want. This is in addition to having the extra freedom and time I now have to devote to our relationships.

I feel very fortunate, and I don't take it for granted. But my values demand that I stand by those "reasonable limits" everywhere in my life. It's the only way it works. For example, my wife and I make our teenage daughters pay for 75 percent of many of the luxury items they want. A pair of designer sunglasses isn't a critical need, so they have to find a way to pay for them and, in the process, to learn the value of money.

The value system I was raised with—the one I also try to impart to my children—is very important. The value of money is an interesting and complicated question and one that my wife and I wrestle with constantly. With three children, currently ranging from age ten to seventeen, we want them to understand that Mom and Dad have worked hard and continue to do so, so we can enjoy the "stuff" we have in our lives.

Side Note: I apply the label "stuff" to almost everything we acquire or do that isn't required to live comfortably. As I become more mature, I can see it all really is just stuff. As the late, great comedian George Carlin so eloquently said, "A house is just a place to keep your stuff while you go out and get more stuff."

As you make your decision whether you start a business or "go corporate," make sure you're meeting the demands of your personal values. I'm going to assume you're up to the task or eager to find out if you are. That's why you're still reading this book. Good. There's more. But you knew that, didn't you?

Self-Discipline

One trait you'll find is shared by all successful members of this "club" is fortitude, otherwise known as self-discipline. We understand that the rewards of going it on your own in business are virtually unlimited—but you have to be prepared for the type of stress and commitment required to think of a viable idea, start a new company, execute a plan to bring the vision alive, and to see success.

In my opinion, most successful small business owners are very self-disciplined. Many have a classic "Type A" personality. They aren't interested in a 9-to-5 schedule with a lunch break at the same time every day.

I believe a lack of self-discipline is the cause of many new small business failures. There's a lot of freedom when you're your own boss. This is one thing that makes starting your own business very attractive. But a lot of people forget that the work still must be done. Success depends a great deal on how you approach the work itself.

It's one thing to have the freedom to go fishing and golfing whenever you want. It's another thing entirely to spend most of your time with your hobbies while you rarely devote any serious energy to making business happen.

Decisions, Decisions

As an entrepreneur, you also need to be prepared to make a lot of decisions. Quickly. With a small business, things tend to move really fast. A business owner needs to be ready to make rapid-fire decisions based on a combination of facts and gut instinct.

Not every decision will be correct, but you still must make a decision—it's part of your job description. I've made plenty of bad entrepreneurial decisions in my career. You might recall my idea to put logos on range golf balls. There were more.

After we sold our credit card processing company, I started another very small business. It was just me, at first—a non-employer business. This enterprise eventually grew into a small business offering working capital to other small and mid-sized businesses. The average loan (or technically called "an advance") was approximately $25,000. This money was used for a variety of purposes, including new equipment, payroll taxes, marketing, and many other needs faced by small businesses.

What I was doing in this business is now known as the cash advance industry. I started out slowly as a part-time business, but I eventually had invested over $100,000 of my own capital into it. Over time, I hired a COO and thirteen employees.

I hope you don't mind if I'm candid here. I hate to admit it, but I didn't keep a close enough eye on the operation. It failed as a result, and it was my failure to follow through that brought it down.

The point is, you must be prepared to make decisions quickly. Right or wrong, it falls on you to keep the company moving, and you can't let the fear of making a wrong decision slow you down or you'll fail anyway.

Decisions in the Slow Lane

Of course, decisions must be made in all positions of most businesses. From what I've seen firsthand, however, the decision-making process is a much longer one in corporate America.

Nothing happens fast there, because you have to write several memos and hold meetings before even a semi-important decision can be made.

I often laugh when I ask my corporate friends how their latest meeting went, and they tell me, in all seriousness, they have to schedule another one—to follow up with the last meeting. That's how it goes: meetings in corporate America are followed by more meetings, which are then followed by more meetings, to hopefully finally come up with a decision of some sort.

The Upside . . .

As the owner of my own company, I can make the decisions as soon as I get the information I need to make them. The decision's on me. I can't pass the buck if things don't go right. Ever. But it's also easy to schedule a meeting with myself. I just need to check my calendar to make sure I'm free!

It's a new level of responsibility that can take some getting used to. But it's also a great feeling knowing that I don't have to deal with layers of bureaucracy to get the job done the way I want to see it.

I don't miss the mindless string of endless meetings, either.

Go It Alone or Don't, but Go!

You might decide to operate a business on your own. You may feel better working with a partner. Whatever you decide, now is the time to get moving if you're going to attain some of the freedom over your life you've been missing.

If you think the commitment and work involved in being in

an SB suits you, get started now. It's good to begin while you're young, and—you know as well as I do—you won't be younger next week or next year. If you haven't settled down yet and still don't have financial and family responsibilities to worry about, it's even better—but it's never too late.

The path will only get more difficult to follow as you get older (unless you're independently wealthy, which does make the journey easier). Greater responsibilities, such as college tuition and all the other things required to provide comfortably for a family, will definitely slow your progress when they kick in.

9:00 A.M.

It's Lonely at the Top— But Have You Seen the View?

> "Always look for the fool in the deal.
> If you don't find one, it's you."
>
> —MARK CUBAN, BUSINESSMAN AND OWNER
> OF NBA'S DALLAS MAVERICKS

I hear two questions all the time: 1) As a small business owner, what's a typical day like? and 2) Isn't it lonely being the boss?

I should say right off, I find the first question certifiably naive. There's no such thing as a typical day when you're an entrepreneur. I probably average sixty to sixty-five hours a week at work (and I've unfortunately had to work in excess of one hundred hours per week throughout my career), but, as I explained at the beginning of this book, I'm always thinking about my business, whatever else it is I might be doing.

This is how it is for most entrepreneurs.

For me, it got so bad that leaving work early used to make me feel self-conscious. Sometimes, I might go play golf with friends or I'd just leave because I felt like leaving early. After all, it is my business. Who cares where I'm going? As long as I'm still responsible for making payroll and keeping the lights on, I earned the right to do as I please.

Still, there were times I'd make up a "white lie." I might say that I was going to a meeting when, in reality, I was just ready to hit the golf course.

This freedom to do what I want is one of the perks I get for going through what it took to build my business. Still, I also maintain a work ethic that I think is part of the blame for my occasional discomfort with taking advantage of freedom.

The point is, there's no typical day in an entrepreneur's life. It's always going to be different, day to day. *Always*. Some weeks might be a bit lighter than others. This is when I have the ability to take off anytime I absolutely need to.

It doesn't always go that way. The reality is, it's not always bliss being the CEO of a small company. In fact, it often sucks.

I definitely want to tell you the whole story—what really goes into building or working in an SB. This is it.

The Good, the Bad, and . . .

When it comes to the second question, make no mistake about it—as an entrepreneur, some days can be long, frustrating, and very lonely. Many times, I just want to forget the whole "enjoy the journey" yoga mantra and get right to the final outcome already. You know, it's kind of like that feeling you get when you're driving all night to get back home, and you're just a half hour outside of town. You keep pushing harder, but you also wish you were there. Now.

I definitely know what it's like. When I started my first company, Mericom Marketing, I was on my own. I had no partners or associates—it was a very small business in every sense of the word, and I was very much alone at the helm.

One of the biggest problems I had was having no one to talk to or bounce ideas off. This experience taught me to be a huge believer in business groups. I'm very fortunate to be involved with three groups that now serve me in different capacities, in addition to the meaningful friendships I've built over the years in my business.

In 1998, I joined Vistage (formerly called TEC). In 2007, I became a member of Young Presidents Organization (YPO). In 2011, I joined Strategic Forum, which is a business group based in South Florida and New York City, and in 2015, I joined the Inner Circle Mastermind. Joining these groups of like-minded and different-minded business leaders with great value systems has truly changed my life on many levels. I feel fortunate for these relationships.

I want to specifically mention one subset of my YPO Group—my "Forum Group." Forum provides me a safe and secure place to share my confidential thoughts with seven Forum brothers and sisters. We meet monthly for four hours, with no hidden agendas, diving into all the different areas of our lives as entrepreneurs and executives—personal, family, and professional. Any topic can be discussed—there is no judging. It's a very comfortable place to visit; plus they are very special people in every sense of the word. I'd like to take this space to thank all of my Forum colleagues by name (using first names only to protect their privacy): Jessica, Joanna, Abe, Naren, John, Tom, and Jorge. I thank each of you for your friendship, business advice, and for serving as my advisory board.

Follow your path. It can be lonely when you're the CEO, but you'll never have to be alone as you launch and build your business—even when your business is you and you alone. But even when you have employees, there will still be plenty of times you feel alone. Groups like the ones I mentioned above—among many others that are available—are a huge help. I strongly recommend you find a group you relate to and join!

Size Doesn't Matter

10:00 A.M.

Don't Be a Freud!

> "Every time you feel yourself being pulled into
> other people's drama, repeat these words:
> Not my circus, not my monkeys."
>
> —POLISH PROVERB

If you're bootstrapping your venture with limited capital, it could be a while before you can start hiring help. You might be tempted to hold off on the added expense and complexity that employees bring to the table. While it's always prudent to work within your budget, you'll need to remain open to the idea of adding employees as soon as possible.

Many entrepreneurs wait too long. Don't be one of them.

You should hope there's a point soon where you need employees. It means you've managed to grow your business as big as you can on your own and there's more growing it can still do with the added help.

To prepare for bringing on this additional help, you also need to develop the ability to hand over a lot of what you normally do yourself now, still working all on your own, to other people. You need to learn to let them do their jobs or fire them if they prove they can't.

And, after you start hiring . . .

Don't Even Think about Becoming the Office Psychologist!

You can't put off adding employees forever, in spite of the added expense and complexity they bring into any business. The right hires at the right time can actually save you money in the long run. They can also make you money. They will definitely help your business grow when the time is right.

However, the truth is, they can also be the cause of much of the additional stress involved in running your business. This truly is one of the biggest decisions entrepreneurs struggle with. It's also often a decision you'll find you're forced to make at some point in your business's growth—so we'd better deal with it right now.

Chew on this a bit: it's great to have people working for you—until it's not.

When you do find you need employees, it's important that you know that managing people will be one of the biggest issues and expenses you'll encounter. Whenever a group of people are gathered together, there will be gossip, goof-offs, and personality conflicts. People seem to naturally create drama. For some reason, this seems to be especially true whenever people are gathered in one place to work. When it starts affecting their work, it becomes your drama.

The Hand That Feeds . . . Gets Bitten

There's no end to the ways employees will make you pay for your kindness. I consider myself to be a very fair person. I enjoy being able to provide a lot of freedom for my employees. However, I do expect them to be at work on time every day, unless they have a vacation day or preplanned event. When they call in sick unexpectedly or have a flat tire—whether what they're saying is true or not—it impacts our overall performance and the company's bottom line.

Still, years ago, a gentleman who worked for us always seemed to call in sick on Mondays and Fridays. I knew he was doing this just to create a long weekend for himself. I would have preferred it if he'd been honest and just asked for the days off when he wanted them. There would still have been a limit to what I'd allow, but I would have accommodated his requests whenever I could. Instead, he chose the path that caused the most drama—for me and for the rest of the team at work—and it had to be stopped.

I also find it comical that whenever I walk through our offices, whether it's near the cubicles or the physical offices, I can always see the computer screens quickly switching from Facebook or other Internet sites or personal Gmail accounts—back to their Word and Excel documents. Some days, it looks almost like a "crowd wave" at a sporting event, with screens switching just as I approach and switching back as soon as I pass.

I understand that people need to do some personal stuff during work hours. But they also can't be doing just personal work from 9 a.m. to 5 p.m. I have to draw the line, and they know it.

My advice to you here is to set your line clearly, then nip everything that goes beyond that line in the bud, as fast as you possibly can, without simply burning the office to the ground. The "scorched earth" approach should be reserved only for the direst of situations.

Of course, I'm kidding here. But trust me, there will indeed be days when simply taking a match to it all feels like a solid approach.

Just remember this, and you'll save yourself a lot of headaches: one of the quickest ways to go crazy is getting involved in the day-to-day rumors and personality conflicts your employees are currently "enjoying." If it doesn't affect business, it's best to let them hash it out themselves.

Hopefully, you've made them understand that fist fighting is considered "over the line." Fire them if the drama can't be controlled. You can't succeed with running your business and trying to be a psychologist for your employees. That's simply not how it works.

How "Quick on the Draw" Should You Be?

The best advice I ever heard to minimize problems with drama at work was to "hire slowly and fire faster." Unfortunately, most entrepreneurs get it completely reversed. However, this one concept is the most valuable piece of advice I've learned as an entrepreneur!

Famous books, such as Jim Collins's *Good to Great,* speak eloquently about getting the right people on the bus and into your organization. People are what differentiate companies. Getting the right people on board is what ensures a strong and, hopefully, successful company. Without great personnel, the odds favor failure.

As a start-up, it's often harder to recruit talented people willing to work within your limited budget who also fit into your culture and belief system. Don't ever let the difficulty of this task press you into hiring the first person who comes along for the job. Do your due diligence before hiring anyone. Take your time ensuring that you've found the perfect fit. Then, honor those special individuals when they join your organization. They're an extension of you, and vice versa.

What if you give someone a shot and it doesn't work out or fit into the culture of your company? Do them, the rest of the team, and any future employees you may hire the honor of setting that person free to seek better positioning elsewhere, quickly and without unnecessary fanfare.

The interaction of the employees within your four walls and outside of the company is always going to be a tricky issue. You want to do all you can to keep drama at a minimum. I advise you to maintain a professional attitude in the office. This is why I don't typically socialize with our staff outside of work, except for occasional bowling parties or a social drink, once per quarter. I feel it helps to maintain a necessary distance, even if it seems stuffy or snobby at times.

Regardless of how that might sound to you, I always try to respect my employees as people first. Still, even at the risk of sounding like I'm Mr. Burns on *The Simpsons*, I simply don't think it's a good idea to be overly friendly with employees outside of the work environment. It's never served me well.

Side Note: I don't promote ever hiring someone on "gut" instinct alone. I learned this lesson the hard way, as you'll read in an upcoming chapter. While it might be okay to spend a few extra dollars on a marketing program based on your gut, you never want to hire a person who will be working inside your organization with you too quickly and without due diligence. You may find, eventually, that you can skip checking regularly into what's going on in every aspect of your business, but, based on my experience, I suggest you have your tentacles in all facets of your business as much as possible. Always. And remember—hire slowly, fire faster.

Welcome to the "Ivory Tower"

Even when you have employees running all over the office doing most of the work, it will always feel lonelier than working for someone else in an office where you can hang around the "water cooler" with all the other employees.

You'll eventually find that it can even be beneficial that you're alone.

However, it's important at this juncture to remember why you started a business in the first place. Until you hire someone to be your COO, you'll want to maintain that position yourself— and that's fine. Don't succumb to the temptation and accept a position as the COP (chief office psychologist). You don't need the added burden of everyone else's problems while you're trying to run a business. You'll find it continually pushes you away from the goals you set out to accomplish when you started your business.

You will feel a bit isolated if you're doing it right. You'll come off to your employees as being almost aloof, but you'll have a firm grip on what's happening in your office and in your business. Know this going in, and you'll be fine.

To accomplish the seemingly impossible task of running a successful small business, you should keep asking yourself if things are working. If they aren't, you need the resolve to take immediate steps to correct the situation. Remember, you're doing this to make a better life for you and your family.

As your company's budget grows, you'll eventually need to learn to let go of all the tasks you were involved with as a solo entrepreneur and hire experienced people to act as employees. Look forward to the day you can replace yourself as COO. When the time finally comes, this can be a lot harder than you might imagine.

Ask Yourself, "Am I Happy?"

> "If you can dream it, you can do it."
>
> —WALT DISNEY, COFOUNDER
> OF THE WALT DISNEY COMPANY

I honestly don't think people dream big enough. I sometimes fail to do this myself. You need to keep your dreams big and maintain a course that keeps you on track to achieve them. It's the entrepreneur's way of doing things.

To do this, you also need to constantly ask yourself if you're happy. It's not an unreasonable thing to ask, and the answer really only needs to be a simple yes or no. There's no qualifying it. Just one word, either way. That's it. "Maybe" isn't an acceptable answer.

That might sound easy. It's not.

The truth is, either you're happy with what's going on in your business—and, more important, in your life—or you're not. If you're honest with yourself and listen to your answer, it's a great barometer for success. You will want to question your progress at every turn, and make sure the people closest to you are doing the same. This will keep you rolling toward success.

Keeping your eye on that big dream is necessary to maintain the passion for what you do and to follow through with everything involved—and passion isn't something you can make up on your own. Again, this is where joining a business group is highly recommended. The right group will be populated by people like you who are also entrepreneurs. They won't be afraid to speak their minds and challenge one another as they help one another grow. This can be your ultimate checkpoint. The truth behind your happiness barometer keeps you on course to the success you dream of attaining.

Is It Really Love?

> "The major value in life is not what you get.
> The major value in life is what you become."
> —JIM ROHN, ENTREPRENEUR, AUTHOR,
> AND MOTIVATIONAL SPEAKER

I'm always pleased when people ask me what I love doing most. I assume they ask this question because, at times, it might seem as if I tackle whatever I do with something that could only be described as a workaholic fervor. However, my answer is always ready for them, and it's always something along the lines of, "I love hanging out with my wife and kids, and playing golf."

I think people are shocked when they don't hear the word "business" in my reply somewhere. The truth is, there's a huge difference between what I truly love doing and growing a business. Can I honestly say I love selling credit card processing to merchants? Did I love having to reprice a merchant in an effort to save the account over a few dollars? No, of course not—especially not when prospective businesses use my pricing just to go back to their existing credit card vendors and have the incumbents match it.

I do love it when I meet and work with small business owners and corporations all over the United States and around the world. It's always fun hearing their stories and forming genuine friendships. I consider it one of the perks of the business I chose to start. And the relationships I've formed have led to another great perk that ties directly into one of my true loves: being invited to their annual corporate golf tournaments.

I do love playing golf, and I consider myself lucky whenever I can play in a golf event with my clients. I've recently received my seventh free golf bag as an outing gift.

Side Note: Golf event organizers should finally learn to stop giving golf bags as gifts. We all already have golf bags. How else did we get our clubs to the course? I could, for example, always use more golf balls instead.

Seriously, it's the people that make work fun for me. The concept that I can earn money for my family and for my employees' families, with no ceiling on my own earnings, drove me to accomplish what I've managed to achieve so far.

There are other perks. Several years ago, we had a better-than-expected year with greater profits than typically experienced. During annual reviews, having the opportunity to give a major bonus to one of our key reports and seeing her break down in tears from happiness was truly one of my most magnificent moments in business.

That was the kind of business moment that completely validates my hard work, if you ask me; rewarding my associates who helped attain my personal goals is always something I relish doing.

What I Really Love about My Business

In truth, I do have a deep and lasting love of the things that make business possible—especially everything that goes into helping to launch a business. I also love the relationships I was able to form over the years while running all of my businesses. However, the thing I love most about having my own business is the freedom it gives me to live life on my own terms. That's it for me. What do I truly love most about being an entrepreneur in one word? Freedom!

The good you can accomplish after going through everything it takes to achieve entrepreneurial success makes it all very well worthwhile. The odds of success are also as good—if not better— than working your way up the corporate ladder to achieve anything similar.

One key to success in your business is maintaining a balance between doing everything you absolutely need to get done and maintaining a solid life outside of your business.

Dancing on the Balance Beam

A lot of people resist the entrepreneurial life because they feel it's going to fill up their time and attention. It's true: building a business will require some crazy hours. I'm sorry to break this news to you. I'm certain I just shattered the hopes and dreams some of you might have had—even though it might be the result of watching too many late-night infomercials telling you how easy it can be to make a fortune in your pajamas at home.

Learning the truth, you might wonder how what I've described is any different from being a workaholic first-year law firm associate. You know—one of those people you hear people whispering about at family gatherings.

I have a good family friend whose son is a first-year associate in a law firm. He works until midnight most nights. I can't even come close to identifying with that kind of schedule anymore. His beats mine for craziness, hands down.

When I was an investment banker, my life was anything but balanced. I was only twenty-one, so it was okay for things to be the way they were—at the time. By comparison, at times, the hours you'll find yourself working to build your own business might make those other high-pressure, big corporate jobs look like a vacation.

But we're all "Type A" people, right? We all like being busy and adding more pressure, don't we? I'm kidding. A bit. Seriously, after the start-up phase, your life will usually become more balanced over time, especially if you hire proper management to help support you. Then your business can start being as balanced as you feel comfortable making it, as long as your business continues to grow and profit.

Too Many People for One Body to Handle

If you recognize yourself in this next story, rethink how you're approaching things.

I'd like to tell you now about my younger brother, Gregg. That's not a typo—my parents named him with two *g's* for some reason. I think they wanted to be different, to make him special, and they felt the extra *g* made the difference.

He's now a labor attorney with his own extremely successful practice. He's professional, anal (in the positive connotation of the word), and totally driven for success. However, for the last twenty years, he's also worked at least ninety hours a week. It's all-consuming. Gregg is a perfectionist, he's very smart, and he feels the need to be involved in all aspects of his law practice.

It seems to be working for him. His firm has achieved a national reputation and continues to attract larger and more sophisticated class action lawsuits. But as his firm continues to grow, it's become increasingly hard for him to have the biggest caseload in the firm while also serving as the rainmaker and administrator and dealing with all the day-to-day issues.

I don't mean to disparage my brother in any way. I just worry about him and hope he makes the right decisions with his practice going forward. I have to wonder . . . can he continue to work those crazy hours for the next twenty years? For example, during our traditional Christmas ski vacation, he spent every chairlift ride making phone calls and negotiating cases with his gloves off—in ten-degree weather. I'm amazed he didn't get frostbite on his hands—and in his brain!

Again I'm half kidding here. Gregg and I are great friends. My parents' greatest wish has always been that we be incredibly close as brothers. Their wish came true.

Another point—I would suggest every family try to have a lawyer in it. You'll save significant money when you need drafting of legal documents or legal advice.

The Balance within the Balance

In spite of the above cautionary tale, also realize there will be periods of time—at all points of building your business and often while running it—when you'll be required to fire up the midnight oil. Most often, this will be when you're trying to close an important deal, launching a new product or service, dealing with deadlines to get a totally new marketing campaign in place or fulfilling a huge order from a major client.

The clock's always ticking when you're running your own business, and the days go by fast. It can wind up requiring more of your time than you'll ever put in working for someone else. Other times, as you get past the start-up phase and begin putting employees in place, you'll find you can arrange things so you have more available downtime. It's a trade-off.

The trick here is to realize this going in and plan for it. Then, adjust your life a bit to accommodate it, and it's not so bad.

1:00 P.M.

Downtime:
Maximizing the Minutes

> "Leadership is an active role; 'lead' is a verb.
> But the leader who tries to do it all is headed
> for burnout, and in a powerful hurry."
>
> —BILL OWENS, POLITICIAN

When you do get some downtime, you want to make sure you take advantage of it with the right kinds of activities to keep your life in balance. As an entrepreneur, you won't necessarily ever have a "schedule"—at least not for a good long while, until you've built out your business. Even then, you'll never be able to simply clock out and forget everything at the same time every day. You also won't have a boss who gets concerned when you start showing signs of burnout—someone who tells you to go take some time to regroup on a beach somewhere . . . on the company card.

Get all that out of your head. Now, just like everything else you'll be doing to run your business, it's all up to you—and nothing will happen if you don't make it happen Then follow through until it does.

Again, I feel like apologizing. I know this can be a hard pill to swallow. Just remember: you wanted to get off the time clock and take control of your life for the opportunity to earn greater income and a sizable net worth.

Manage Your Downtime

One thing I've done in an effort to provide my brain with downtime is take up yoga. I recommend it highly. It's an hour that allows you to purely relax and shut down. You get to do some stretching, too—which is great as we all get older and less flexible.

This isn't always easy for me. Remember—my brain is always mulling something over. Usually, even when I'm enjoying some necessary downtime, my mind is still spinning away. Yoga helps me give this one part of my body the break it dearly needs. If you don't take up yoga, do whatever it is you would enjoy—perhaps meditation or maybe just taking a few long, quiet breaths throughout the day—to achieve similar relaxation for your mind, for at least a bit.

I did get yelled at once by my yoga teacher for sneaking a peek at my iPhone during the class. So much for taking one hour to relax, I guess.

It's important that you do. You'll never be too busy for it, because so little is required to do it. So . . . no excuses!

The "No Business" Zone

You also want to do whatever is possible to keep your business from encroaching on your home life—especially your family time. We have a rule at our house that there are no cell phones allowed at the dinner table. Without this rule, it's far too easy to see everyone spend the entire meal staring at small glowing screens, checking email, texting, or surfing the Internet instead of relating with one another and catching up on how our respective days went.

I'm the only one who can get away with breaking this rule, which I candidly do whenever a random, yet important, thought comes into my mind. I do still enter them into my phone whenever they happen . . . even during dinner with the family. I often get caught and yelled at by my kids—and they're right. Then I'm stressed, thinking about the note I was going to enter, trying to retain it in my brain until I can type it in following dinner.

Whew! It can turn into a vicious cycle. See why I need yoga?

A good relationship with family begins with looking each other in the eye and having a real conversation at least once a day. When we're together, we also try to make sure our discussion is about something other than work. That can wait. Kids need to talk about their day at school. They need to hear their parents actually speak to each other as well. For this reason, dinnertime isn't the time to whip out phones or start rattling off the business stuff currently going on in my head—that is, when I'm home for dinner and not in a meeting or traveling for business. It's the times I'm away that make family dinnertime even more valuable.

Whatever it is, it can wait for just a little while.

This also goes for time spent in the car. You know as well as I do that texting and driving is totally unacceptable. Nothing's that important that it can't wait until you pull over. I've been guilty of this in the past, but now that I have two teenage girls who are driving, I've stopped—and not only because it's a terrible example for them. I realize now, as I hope you and everyone else does, that texting while driving can be the difference between life and death. I simply don't do it anymore.

The texting can wait for the passengers, too, if you ask me. There can be some excellent conversations to enjoy on the ride to and from school, or just during those few minutes before the kids get out of the car at sports practice. I can't stand when my children are always texting when I drive them to and from their activities. As I like to tell them, "I'm not your chauffeur" (even though I guess I really am!).

Even if you live alone and work in an "office" set up in the corner of your living room—establish boundaries between where you work and where you live. Set up a barrier of some kind. Establish a "no-work zone" everywhere in your home except where that office is set up.

This might seem trivial. It's not. Do it.

Friends Are Vitally Important

It's also important that you take time out from work to focus on your marriage and your core friendships. Spend some memorable time together. It's so easy for a business owner to work all the time. There's always something going on that could benefit from your attention, so this takes some willpower and determination.

You'll be a better person for it, and your business will be better because of it.

Friends are also an integral part of a good work-life balance to enhance the value of your downtime. You should try, as often as possible, to get together with people you don't work with. It's honestly better if they don't even have a real understanding of what you do for a living.

One way to do this is joining groups that might be interested in something totally different from what you do. Perhaps a baking class. Maybe art class. Or tennis lessons. Whatever it is— these are outside of the business groups you belong to and have nothing to do with what you do for a living. It will broaden your mind and give you something else to think and talk about during downtime besides work.

Show Your Appreciation

Finally, get involved in a charity. Nothing makes you realize and truly appreciate how good you have it until you see people who are struggling to get by day to day. It doesn't matter what their issues are, you should make an effort to give back to your community in some way, because giving back is critical to your own balanced life. There's no shortage of organizations that will welcome your help.

I was raised in a very charitable and philanthropic home; my parents were leaders of many causes, including school, religious, and civic involvements. As a teenager, I vividly remember my mom and dad being out many nights organizing functions, calling friends to join upcoming functions, and basically just being involved.

That's the word that echoes in my mind: "involved." Just do something. Pick a cause—something you feel an affinity toward—and make a difference.

I know I can always do more, and, many times, I feel guilty that I don't. But I'm proud that my wife and I have chosen a few causes that we're passionate about and jumped in with both feet.

By all means, get the whole family involved in your charitable downtime, too. It's important for children to have a deep understanding of how good their lives are, compared to others who are less fortunate, and how hard it is for many kids when their parents are struggling to supply just the basics. It's also a great way to spend quality time with your family.

I can't imagine a much better way to make my downtime matter than by helping out with a worthy charity. The friends we associate with also tend to be charitable. Being charitable is very nice, but one of the problems is saying no to some of them. All causes are terrific in their own right, but, at some point, it's virtually impossible to get involved—from a time and financial standpoint—with all of them. I'll always give to any friend who asks me to support a worthy cause. Some charitable functions I'm invited to, however, may cost hundreds or even thousands of dollars, and it's just not feasible to do everything. So it's important that you also know when to say no.

Incorporate these kinds of activities and considerations into your downtime plans now, so you keep from entering into the "workaholic zone."

Don't think for a minute you can't ever wind up there. Being a workaholic is a creeping problem. Most of us who are business owners have to combat the urge to work all the time. Quality downtime is crucial to long-term success with any business or job, and, when you choose to be an entrepreneur, it's all up to you.

A balanced life is a happy life, and that's why you're looking to own a business—right?

Which Is It:
A Business or a Job?

> "If opportunity doesn't knock—
> build a door."
>
> —MILTON BERLE, COMEDIAN AND ACTOR

If you're looking at building or buying a business, it's good to know if it's actually just going to be a job or a real business. At first, it might seem like a simple matter of semantics. However, when it comes to finding a great opportunity for advancement and growth, owning a business is the whole enchilada. It's the goal to go after. It can help make your dreams of living on your own terms a reality while you escape the tedium of a 9-to-5 job that's capable of sending even the most dedicated person into autopilot.

It's an excellent mental barometer you can use when deciding whether you should pursue a business concept. Just ask the question, "Is it a job, a business, or an opportunity?" It's important that you ask this question and understand the differences between all three. This will help keep your sights set on the goal you're shooting for—a successful, sustainable business.

Job Spotting

Visualize what a 9-to-5 job actually looks like. This will help you see whether a possible business you're looking into might turn out to be something similar. There's nothing wrong with a job . . . many people are perfectly happy with a business that runs at that level. Most, however, are looking for just about anything but a job. Either way, visualizing the typical 9-to-5 workday will help you.

I've already shown you that the typical day for an entrepreneur is essentially impossible to nail down. Well, the typical day of a person who has a job is much easier to map out in pretty amazing detail. It's so much simpler that it can quickly start to feel routine. While this does appeal to some people, escaping it is one of the major reasons why many people leave the workforce to start their own businesses.

I have friends who work the 9-to-5 day who describe their day as follows—perhaps you've experienced it for yourself:

9:00 a.m.   Arrive at the office. Never be early or late. Arrive right on time.

9:00 a.m.–   Get settled at the desk, have some coffee, and chat
10:00 a.m.   with coworkers about what happened in the hours since you last saw them. Read a few emails—some of them might even be work-related.

10:00 a.m.– Do some actual work, with a few interruptions to use
12:00 p.m.   Google and take a quick peek at personal emails.

12:00 p.m.–12:30 p.m.	Start winding things down in preparation for lunch.
12:30 p.m.–1:30 p.m.	Lunch.
1:30 p.m.–2:00 p.m.	Take a bathroom break and prepare to get back to work.
2:00 p.m.–4:00 p.m.	Take time to work hard and stay focused. It's also probably time for an internal office meeting. Maybe two, if the first one's too short.
4:00 p.m.–5:00 p.m.	Get ready to leave for the day.
5:00 p.m.	Head home for the day.

Of course, I'm being a bit facetious here, but I don't think the source of this satire, at its core, is all that far off from the truth. Employees work for companies, and they get their salaries as long as they work at an expected pace and spend a predetermined length of time doing it. If this is okay with you, but you'd like to call your own shots, you might do well building a business that, ultimately, is a job.

A real business, on the other hand, requires that entrepreneurs earn their money every day. Everything they do has to pay the freight, cover the bills, and—hopefully—leave some money for the CEO to take home and live on.

This concept of earning the money every step of the way starts over again every month. Then over again. Year after year, for better or worse.

A job generally means you're out the door at 5:00 p.m.—

or whenever quitting time actually might be. Your work is done for the day. Building a business means your brain never stops working—even when you're trying not to work. You're always thinking of ways to improve things and sell more, keeping an eye out for new opportunities. You have to use a mental approach to your future and think big in a different way than most people working in jobs do.

I'll use a sports analogy for illustrative purposes: golfers and tennis players must earn their weekly income by winning tournaments. If they don't make the cut, they don't get paid for that particular effort. This type of payment scheme is more entrepreneurial than, say, athletes who play team sports such as basketball and football. Those sports are more corporate in many ways. These athletes are guaranteed a salary. They're part of a team environment. But, of course, they must produce—on and off the field—to continue to earn their pay.

A Big Case of the "Likes"

Many times, people around the water cooler (that might sound trite; it is what it is) will state, "You must like the industry your business is in." I find that to be a crazy statement. A lot of people really like sports or music or the entertainment industry. However, how many people actually get to work in these industries? Not many, that's for sure—and most are employees who don't make anywhere near the kind of money you were probably thinking of when you imagined the glamour these industries hold.

My wife's first and only corporate job after graduating from college was for the NBA, where she was working when I met her for our blind date, as I mentioned earlier. And, as you already know, she didn't play for one of the teams, but she did work just as hard to make her way up through the corporate ladder. Her final position was director of marketing.

I love Jill for all her great qualities, but it sure didn't hurt having the opportunity to attend lots of basketball games, the Olympics, and other perks her position afforded us. Although to an outsider her job sounded amazing with all the sports bene-fits that went with it, work is still work. As she likes to say, "Yes, it was fun attending many New York Knicks basketball games (especially when they were competitive—unlike the 2014–15 sea-son), but it's a very different experience going to those games with friends and family from entertaining clients and having to be 'on' the entire evening."

I do believe it's better if you have a love for the product/ser-vice you're offering—but I don't think it's critical for success. You do, however, need to be in love with the idea of doing things for yourself, controlling your future, and taking pride in your efforts. Enough so that you're more than willing to build the vehicle that will take you there.

Avoid the Clown Car
and Step into the Right Vehicle for You

Many people have different aspirations, interests, and skill sets. For example, one person might aspire to a 9-to-5 job at AT&T. They might be perfectly happy going home at the end of a shift, not thinking more of it again until the next morning when he or she has to be back to work.

If that's what you want, there are plenty of opportunities out there. As of this writing, the job market appears to be improving.

Another person might be interested in having their own AT&T store, with a vast selection of shiny mobile devices to sell. They want most to take advantage of the opportunity an AT&T store has to offer—and one store will do.

Then there's a person who isn't happy being an employee or owning just one store. This person wants to be a multi-unit franchise AT&T owner and keep on amassing stores for their empire. They're aiming for a real business where the sky's the limit.

None of these aspirations are wrong. They each just highlight the differences in how people think and what they view as success in business. Assessing what it is that determines success for you is something you'll find yourself doing a lot as an entrepreneur. Get used to it. Maybe the employee in the AT&T store is perfectly happy punching out at the end of the day to then pursue an actual passion that has nothing to do with iPhone, Android, or Samsung mobile devices. The person who wants one store may be very content making a living that way and is happy to keep it small for any number of reasons. The business owner who aspires to own lots of stores will be happy as well and likely will always on the lookout for the next big deal. It's how that particular person ticks.

That's why you want to fully understand how you tick before you make the decision to embark on launching a business of your own. It's almost more important than understanding the business you're thinking about starting.

I will say that owning a business is great, when it works—and totally awful when it doesn't. That's the way the life of an entrepreneur really goes. Stick around. There's some stuff I still have to share with you that will surely get your attention.

It certainly grabbed mine.

Will You Start a Company or Buy a Business?

> "As long as you're going to be thinking anyway, think big."
>
> —DONALD TRUMP, CHAIRMAN AND PRESIDENT
> OF THE TRUMP ORGANIZATION

There are several ways you can accomplish your goal to become an entrepreneur, including but not limited to:

○ You can start something from scratch—with or without a partner.

○ You can buy an existing business with the help of a business broker, advisor, or other expert.

○ You can start working at a company and, over time, earn the confidence of the owners. You might—perhaps, eventually—be allowed to participate in a buy-in for cash or sweat equity, becoming a minority partner with a chance to fully own a controlling interest.

The avenue you pick is up to you. Which path you take will depend on your personal goals and how risk-averse you happen to be.

Starting something from scratch—especially on your own—can be overwhelming. As I mentioned earlier, I've done this a few times. Not having someone in your business to work with and to bounce ideas back and forth with can make getting your business launched a more challenging experience. Partners can help here—a lot. However, I don't believe equal partnerships work. In my opinion, someone must own 51 percent, and you should probably try to be that person.

Buying an existing business or becoming a minority partner will take money—and not all opportunities are created equally. You want to make sure the business you're considering is financially stable, has a proven track record, and already has established clients. It's a very bad idea to get involved in a business that's totally dependent on one big client. Losing that "big fish" can easily hurt the overall financial stability of the company if no one's taken the time to create a larger client base before they're gone.

Also—and I can't say this enough—make sure the company is in a growing industry. The thing you think you're passionate about might not be the "in" thing at the moment for enough people "out there." Plowing along trying to make an unpopular idea profitable can lead you to financial disaster. Finally, technology can render a business an anachronism. It's also a lot to keep up with, if technology is what you choose to sell.

Buying into a franchise is certainly possible, and there are plenty of excellent opportunities available in the market. In fact, most major cities host franchise conferences where you can look at hundreds of opportunities all in one place. A good friend of mine bought one of the first Subway franchises and has, over the past thirty-seven years, become the largest area developer in the world. He had the foresight to envision Subway growing, but I'm not sure even he could have envisioned Subway having over 43,000 locations worldwide by 2015.

I didn't invent the industry of credit card processing. Instead, I realized there was a proven model for the business, got in—when, in my opinion, it was still early in the industry—and then went big. I hired people to manage the different areas, and I kept working to make our network of merchants and our relationships grow bigger.

The Family Business: Ties That Bind . . . or Blind

"You have to respect your parents. They are giving you an at-bat. If you're an entrepreneur and go into the family business, you want to grow fast. Patience is important. But respect the other party . . ."

—GARY VAYNERCHUK, ENTREPRENEUR, AUTHOR, AND SPEAKER

When it comes to working with family members in my business, I consider myself very lucky. I had the most positive experience working with my dad and our mutual friend, Tony, as we developed and grew our merchant services business.

Unfortunately, I've talked to too many other people who weren't as lucky working with their families. All too often, it ended up with everyone filing lawsuits against one another. The rifts in the family dynamic from those experiences never fully heal. Sometimes, the family counseling and therapy sessions cost more money than the actual start-up cost of the business they're fighting about!

I'd like to share an experience my dad had in his first business: Majestic Industries, Inc. was founded by my great grandfather. In the early 1900s, the business sold packaging to small stores. My grandfather expanded the business to make file folders for the U.S. government and, unfortunately, at the age of fifty-four years old, died of a massive heart attack. So, when my father was in his early twenties, he suddenly became the president of a small business with fewer than ten employees. His sister, a psychotherapist, inherited the other 50 percent of the business, as determined by the will.

Although this happened years ago, my father recalls the story like it happened yesterday.

While my father loved his sister, neither her skill set nor desire was in running a business (in all fairness, my father also had no clue about how to provide psychological counseling). My father also wasn't prepared to have an equal partner—family or no family. He wasn't comfortable checking with someone on every decision and sharing the financial success with someone who was doing none of the work. After some difficult conversations, my father and his sister/partner finalized negotiations. A lump sum payout was arranged, and my father became the sole owner of Majestic moving forward.

The company was successful. It grew from a small number of employees to a staff of 225, with Fortune 500 companies being its major market. Through acquisitions, many more synergistic products were manufactured. It was making money and growing—all good things for any company. My father met all types of challenges and recognized it was time to sell his business and enjoy the fruits of his efforts.

As a twelve-year-old, I wasn't privy to all the conversations between my parents, but I do know my father decided to change his career path. He sold his interest in his company to a business partner. His partner grew the business even larger through organic growth and by continuing with acquisitions. All that growth, however, required significant financial leverage and borrowing. Unfortunately, the business was eventually so leveraged with debt that his former partner was ultimately forced to close its doors.

My dad was truly out of the business by that point, but it still took a huge emotional toll on him when it closed. It hurt him to see the business he helped build go into bankruptcy.

Running a business in a financially prudent manner is critical. Too often, business owners don't take the time for monthly reviews to see if they're making or losing money. Although this concept seems so simple, I'm confident that many SB owners don't focus on this core competency. Think about it in your own situation—do you really know if you made money last month?

Crazy but True!

Another family business experience I had was when my wife joined Charge Card Systems. After the birth of our first daughter, it was no longer feasible for her to continue working for the NBA (and I, unfortunately, was now going to lose my basketball ticket and sports perks connection). She'd hoped to work flex hours, switching between time in the New York City office a few days per week and working from home in New Jersey with Fridays off. But this wasn't meant to be—for many reasons.

We were excited about working together. After nearly eleven years at the League office and the many solid relationships she had built, we believed many of her sports relationships could potentially become processing clients of ours. We felt it would help Charge Card Systems gain a foothold with working with sports leagues, sponsors, and other businesses connected to the field of sports and entertainment.

As director of promotions for the NBA, it was rare that her phone calls weren't returned within twenty-four hours. Of course, she thought this would carry over into her new job as director of sales for my company. I think the "director" title was more powerful when she was working for David Stern, the former NBA Commissioner, than when working for me. In working with her corporate advertisers—including McDonalds, Gatorade, and other Fortune 100 corporations—the small business world turned out to be a vast contrast to the NBA. It wasn't as easy as she thought it was going to be. Suddenly, she saw that her prospects weren't so quick to return her calls despite their past relationship.

She also suffered from what I call "corporate syndrome," requiring that everything be sent by FedEx. After our FedEx bill skyrocketed, I asked her what was going on. She told me it was because the client asked her to send materials overnight. It was hard for her to understand this was now our money and not the NBA's. I told her to ask clients for their FedEx account numbers if they thought they had to have materials the next day. That way, they could pay the excessive delivery fees instead of us. It turned out our clients were surprisingly willing to receive their materials by regular mail if the faster method was on their nickel.

The point to remember is, there are a lot of moving parts in a business. When you add the dynamic of a family or close friend working into your business, the results can be more complex and definitely more unpredictable than they already are.

Believe me—those discussions I had with my wife early on were a lot more difficult than they would have been if it had been another person filling the position.

Family or Not—It's All about the Skill Sets

If family or friends will be joining you in your business, it's good that they each bring skill sets to the team that are needed to strengthen the company. My dad, our partner, and I each had different skill sets, which added to our overall strength as a solid management team. My father enjoyed negotiating contracts, proofing legal agreements, and nurturing our big partnerships; Tony had a sense for the numbers and financial accountability and was a natural salesman; and I had a strategic vision for the business and worked with our sales partners and our local and national merchants.

Together, we were a formidable team. We were all in sync, sharing stories and debating the best way to grow our business every step of the way. With different personalities and skill sets at play, somebody within the organization still needs to be able to make the final and tough decisions to help propel the company forward. Feedback's great, but—whether you use a democratic consensus, an advisory board, or you're the sole decision-maker—somebody must ultimately make the final decision.

You won't always be right. This is why making decisions is, many times, the hardest part of the process.

We were a three-executive "family"—even though Tony isn't a blood relative. We felt like family in almost every sense of the word as we spent our years building the company from the ground up. Although my father was obviously my senior, there were many times when I agreed with Tony's ideas and sided with him. It was Tony, after all, who first came to my dad with the idea about credit card processing.

We were all three equals in every way. The great thing about three executives who are anything but shy working together as equals is, ultimately, we always collectively achieved the best decision based on the facts at hand.

In addition to their capital investment, I also thank my father and Tony for their strategic advice, guidance, knowledge, and—ultimately—for their friendship, all of which were priceless during our partnership.

I'll forever be grateful.

Get Your Networking ROT

> "The currency of real networking
> is not greed, but generosity."
>
> —KEITH FERRAZZI, CEO OF FERRAZZI GREENLIGHT

Did I mention the importance of networking? Why, yes—I think I did! I ask because I'd be remiss if I let you head into the entrepreneurial world without a discussion about the importance of creating networks and developing new relationships. I'd also like to share a few tips for doing it the right way.

As I'm writing this, I recently returned from an industry conference, so the concept of networking has been on my mind. It reinforced the fact that networking, when done properly, is incredibly powerful. Simply put, there's no better way to grow your business.

But what do I really mean by "networking"?

We hear the term often. People who effectively use networking in a positive way seem to always enjoy the greatest returns. But, to accomplish these kinds of results, they don't just network—the networking they do also follows a plan.

Networking isn't like reading a financial statement where the return on investment (ROI) is the overriding concern in the transaction. Networking involves what I like to refer to as a return on time (ROT). This should be any business owner's paramount concern when choosing networking groups for relationship-building. An easy way to remember this is that anything you ignore over time will ROT.

Making networking truly pay off is all about your time and where you spend it. Probably the most frustrating part of networking is deciding where to spend that time and maintaining patience with the process.

For relationships to grow, people have to first become genuinely comfortable with you. It doesn't happen overnight.

Understand that there's a degree of risk when a fellow entrepreneur provides you with an introduction in these groups . . . which is how your network grows. They're already a part of that other person's network. They've already spent the time to build a relationship with them. That relationship could be jeopardized if the hand-off goes badly.

However, once they're confident in your abilities and the qualities you bring to the table, they won't hesitate to help you expand your network. They're also helping their network when they do, and they're always eager to do that. It just takes time to get to that point and have others share their "tribe" of loyal followers with you.

Plan to attend networking meetings all the time. Be seen. Nurture friendships and make people comfortable with you. What seems like a waste of your time one month can easily lead to new business six months down the road—the kind of new business that will carry your enterprise to new levels over time.

Who Hid the "Instant Networking"?

That's the nasty truth. This stuff takes time. There's no jar of "Instant Networking" you can pull out of the cupboard, pour into water, and stir. And a lot of that time won't feel productive. It's not as easy to keep a scorecard or directly track the ROI from this process. You'll do best to focus only on your ROT to determine the best application of what time you do have to devote to the effort.

People are almost always irritated, for example, by the person who will lunge for the lead and run with it, never to return the favor. Many years ago, a gentleman who had founded a property and casualty insurance company joined a networking group I was in. Within just a few days of an initial breakfast meeting, this newcomer called each member, asking for new leads. This is not how you start your first week within a new networking relationship. The end for him was both simple and predictable: he was politely asked to leave the group before the next meeting.

One of the most effective networkers I ever encountered was a guy who seemed to be everywhere. During networking time at conferences and meetings, he always came to me, introduced himself, and gave me his business card. What he didn't do was ask me to give him business or to call him with leads. Instead, he'd always say, "If there's anything I can ever do to help you with potential leads or contacts, please let me know."

Was he giving something away for free? Was he being genuine? Who knows? But he was giving and not just looking to receive. He was also growing his business properly within the networking process. He understood that you never know when that special contact is going to happen—it may be on the initial meeting, by pure luck, or it might take several years—but it will happen. It is called the "law of reciprocity" where people instinctively want to help others who have helped them in the past. It's very powerful, and it's real and true. Think about your own life experiences, whether personal or business related.

If it doesn't happen, it's most likely your fault.

When you're networking, remember that it's important to follow up on any introductions you receive through your network. Although this sounds obvious, I'm amazed when people don't do this—and I'm pretty careful when I refer my connections I've amassed over the years. If I offer a connection, I want to ensure that the person will follow up and make a good presentation.

I view anyone I refer to my network as an extension of me, and I'm very careful when I introduce anyone into that network. I really don't want people in my network who fail to follow up or who don't present themselves well. However, I do think at least some of these failures come from pure laziness. I don't need that in my network, either.

I recommend you make this a full-time effort before you even get started . . . while you're still thinking about starting a business. Then, maintain it long after you've started one.

You should also mix things up a bit in your networking. During my many years of founding companies, the one suggestion I always make to our sales people is that they join a wide variety of groups.

Your Competitors Can Also Be Your Network

I've also seen far too many people get overly concerned about speaking with and sharing information with competitors in their respective industries—within these groups and everywhere else. They point to this paranoid delusion as their reason for being wary of networking.

Of course, you're never asked to share confidential information when you network. You can. When you do, you could just learn even more from your friends and others within your industry. But you don't have to.

Two of my best friends are my direct competitors in the credit card industry. We all have the greatest respect for one another and would never attempt to steal accounts. It's wonderful having friends in the same industry to share war stories and advice with. We can also have candid conversations about the business itself. With a market of approximately twenty million potential merchants, it doesn't bother me if I lose one or two here and there to competitors. There are plenty of customers to go around for all of us. The chances are good that there are plenty of clients to go around for your business, too.

You shouldn't worry about competitors when you network. If you're at all concerned, just look for ways you can make what you sell and how you follow up each sale uniquely yours. Your customers will remain yours when you do, and competitors won't be able to touch you.

I've learned an interesting fact from many of my clients: customers also have a hard time finding great vendors! One expression that's stuck with me over the years is, "Clients would rather buy an average product or service from an extraordinary company than buy an extraordinary product from a bad company." To rephrase that, there are many competitive products, and clients want to buy from companies that provide great service and value their relationships.

It's my belief that expressing concern about your competition exemplifies the fact that you don't have any confidence in your relationships—those you form with your customers and with your competitors. When I go to an industry trade show, I don't view anyone there as competitors or the enemy. I consider all of them my contemporaries.

I think it's very helpful to have a network of trusted advisors who also happen to be your competitors. After all, without a solid network, the odds are greatly stacked against success for you.

Seriously—just get over it! It's very unlikely your idea is so original that no one else ever thought of it before. If no one else is doing it, there might also be a reason. Lots of healthy competition in an industry niche shows you that there's potentially a healthy market still awaiting your entry.

NO Excuses: There Are More Networking Possibilities Than Ever Before!

I also like social media for networking. It's very helpful when it's used correctly. Prior to accepting requests on LinkedIn or other websites, I spend a quick moment to check whether these people have at least some affinity for my profession or they're simply accepting every person they can find into their personal circle of contacts. Many people want to reach that magical number of 500 "friends" on their LinkedIn status so they don't feel so inferior when others search their name to see they only have a handful of contacts.

I also feel that email is one of the best ways to find and reach people. It takes away the excuse of, "Hey, I tried to get in touch, but you weren't in."

I'm also a big proponent of the thank-you note—a lost art of communication. If you can't find the time to write a simple thank you email, then sign up for an Internet portal that, with a simple click of the mouse, will send out email postcards the following day.

With all this readily available technology today, there's simply no excuse for not touching base with potential clients and people you want in your network. Clearly, we live in an amazing age with access to more resources for networking than ever before. Used properly, you can take your networking to levels unheard of just ten to fifteen years ago.

I Put My Bookkeeper in Jail (No Kidding!)

> "Trust is like blood pressure. It's silent, vital to good health, and if abused, it can be deadly."
>
> —FRANK SONNENBERG, AUTHOR OF
> *FOLLOW YOUR CONSCIENCE*

I told you this was going to be different type of book. Real talk. Take a break if you need it. You might want to fix yourself a drink. I have a story for you now that'll make you want something to calm your nerves as you watch it unfold.

As I mentioned earlier, my first company following Lehman was Mericom. This company was fortunately growing its client base and making money. I reached the point when I needed to hire my first employee, which was a big step for me, as it is for any entrepreneur still in the formative years.

After many interviews, Lisa was hired. I won't use her last name. The reason why will, unfortunately, be painfully obvious soon.

I'll never forget Lisa—and not just because she was my first employee. Believe me, I now wish I could forget her. When I hired Lisa, I was quite honestly happy to have anyone join the company. I needed an assistant to help me with the phones, light book-keeping, and other random "stuff." During the interview process, Lisa mentioned she was good with numbers and could help with accounting functions as the company continued to grow.

Stellar!

Lisa came on board. Suddenly, I was running a two-person business. The size of my company had officially doubled that day—from a very, very small one-person business to a small business of two people. Hey—double is double!

As the business grew, I was spending the majority of my time growing the top line sales, constantly selling, and hiring more salespeople. The life of the small business owner is all about time management and using your day to your best advantage. Using her background and comfort with numbers, Lisa started handling the daily accounting issues I no longer had time to manage.

I soon allowed my one-person bookkeeping department (that's a joke) to handle the payables and receivables. This meant Lisa was, at this point, opening monthly bank statements to cross-reference the numbers and ensure that they made sense. I still had a CPA accounting firm do my annual taxes, but Lisa was great with just about everything else.

Her help allowed me to focus on my strongest skill set of selling and marketing the business to new customers. She was self-directing and helped run the internal business functions efficiently.

Tainted Trust

I trusted her. My wife trusted her. She even babysat my young children many weekends when our regular babysitter was busy.

"Trust" is an interesting word. It means everything when you're running a small business. Whom do you trust? Your lawyer? Your accountant? Nobody? Everybody?

I came to rely on Lisa a lot over the first few years of our business relationship. I was also aware, at that point, that she took a real leap of faith when she joined me in my business, too. However, I eventually allowed her to become so insulated, with no checks and balances, that she was too critical within my organization. To be totally honest, I didn't enjoy doing the accounting functions, so I happily adopted a casual attitude toward them after Lisa willingly stepped in.

This was the perfect setup for something bad to happen. It did.

Like many businesses, Mericom had a corporate credit card. We used it whenever possible to earn points on our purchases. Plus it afforded me a thirty-day float on our business expenses. We often spent tens of thousands of dollars on merchandise for our clients' projects. Using that card paid off nicely, as the points often covered my flights and hotel for business trips as well as other business expenses.

In the first months of Lisa's employment, I would open the bills each month and carefully review the line items to make sure they matched. I was completely anal about it. However, the business was growing, and, as I got busier, Lisa began handling the payments pretty much unchecked.

Her payments were always on time, but I did continue to spot-check the bill—for a while. Everything was always just fine, so I eventually gave her complete control over the accounting.

Free . . . with Consequences

I was a free man! I had additional time to grow the company, meet new clients, and get new vendors. It was a great feeling to divide and conquer, uninhibited by all the mundane chores Lisa was handling so adeptly for me.

Or, at least, I thought that's what she was doing—until I found out differently, about two years later.

That's when I came to the office one Sunday, intent on cleaning up my desk and writing a proposal for a prospective client. That's when I happened to see a credit card bill on Lisa's desk. I don't know what made me open it, but I did.

The first thing I saw were lots of charges from vendors I'd never heard of. This was odd, because I knew all of our vendors' names. They called me often and sent new product samples all the time. I was completely bewildered.

I wasn't sure what to do. Was there a mistake? Yes! It had to be a mistake. Lisa loved me. She babysat my kids, and we were in this journey together.

My trip to the office went from a few hours to an all-nighter. By the time I was done, I'd estimated that, over thirty-six months, she'd stolen over $150,000 from the company.

How did she do it? It was frighteningly simple. She'd created partnerships with third-party vendors who, in turn, created dummy invoices that our company paid. Lisa split the profits with them.

I was totally despondent. I was embarrassed to tell my wife what I'd just discovered. I was the victim, but it was also all my fault. I had weeks of sleepless nights following the revelation, because I knew I'd let my guard down. I'd relaxed my grip. I thought I'd found a reliable solution that enabled me to spend the time I needed growing my business—and it was growing. But I failed to set up a system to check on what was being done and follow it through. I'd proceeded without first at least planning how I would proceed moving forward.

I missed the mark when it comes to hitting the small business-planning bull's-eye. I let my employees and especially my family down in the process.

Every time I thought about the money that had just evaporated into thin air, I was stressed beyond words. I was eating terribly and lost all motivation to work out. I didn't want to see my friends. My wife and I stopped going to restaurants for dinner on Saturday nights. I was avoiding work and ignoring phone calls from vendors and clients. I was in a funk and hated how I felt.

This was all because I trusted someone too much and took my eye off the ball so I could focus on the part of the business I liked most and was best doing. I totally screwed up!

It was an extremely expensive and vital lesson in my business journey. I'm sharing this experience in the hope that it never happens to you. I want you to learn not to be naive when running your business. In the end, it's your business and your money. Always.

Since this difficult episode in my business career took place, I've unfortunately heard similar stories of theft and deception from other business owners. In hindsight, looking back on this story, there's obviously a fine line you must walk between micromanaging your people and letting them be free to run their respective divisions.

Crime and Punishment

If you're wondering what became of Lisa, the outcome was pretty straightforward. I went to the police that very night. They got a warrant to search her apartment and found about $50,000 worth of sports memorabilia that she'd purchased with my money.

Since she'd transacted sales over state lines, the FBI was brought in to handle the case. I couldn't believe that I was now working with FBI agents, who were incredibly smart. Their forensic accounting skills were incredible as they tracked down the money to determine if any had been sent to offshore bank accounts. It was like watching a movie unfold. Unfortunately, I was the lead actor in this film.

Over several months, law enforcement traced most of her spending activities, and she was eventually sentenced to twenty-two months in jail. It felt to me like she'd gotten away with a slap on the wrist. But I also received restitution! Lisa was ordered to pay $100,000 back to me over her lifetime. I'll never truly understand how restitution works, but given that she now earns a nominal salary after being released from jail, the courts will only allow her to make small payments so that she can still afford the basic necessities of life while paying down her debt to me.

Assuming she's now earning approximately $30,000 annually, my total restitution payments over the past fifteen years have approached no more than $1,000. If I'm lucky, I might receive another $1,000 in the next twenty years. It does pay for golf balls, if nothing else!

Talk Is Not Necessarily Cheap

Sometimes being in business is just plain expensive, and you simply can't prepare for costly unforeseen issues. For example, I recently purchased a list of business phone numbers for our lending business call center. It contained 10,000 corporate names and phone numbers. It cost $2,000 because it was a targeted database of potential prospects.

When it comes to cold-calling, the rule is that companies are only allowed to call businesses—not consumers. By mistake, one of the numbers in our list was an individual person's cell phone—not a physical business landline. Without going into too much detail, my company was served with a lawsuit that, in the end, cost me $40,000—between legal fees for my California attorney (being that I was served from a California plaintiff) and payment to my "extortionist."

It was clearly extortion. Our research indicated the plaintiff had taken these actions several times before. In the end, however—even though I knew I was correct—I had to defend myself, and the payout for legal fees and the plaintiff were a cost of doing business.

Learn from my experiences. When compiling your annual budgets, make sure you include a line item for "miscellaneous expenses." Unfortunately, it can turn out to be a real number you must deal with at the end of the year. It's always best to be conservative when preparing your budgets, but don't skimp here. It can always be added to next year's budget, if you escape unforeseen calamity for the twelve months previous.

I promise you: unexpected expenses will pop up.

Still, I've been fortunate. Bankruptcy has never been on the radar—even after blows like the ones I've just detailed. Bankruptcy is always a very real possibility, however. Sometimes, it can even be a useful tool for struggling businesses. Still, it's always better to first tell everyone exactly what happened and try to work out an equitable deal than it is to let the courts remove you from the responsibility. The best advice I can deliver here is don't listen to me—seek professional help for these matters!

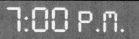

Intentions Aren't Outcomes

> "Any business plan won't survive its first
> encounter with reality. The reality will always
> be different. It will never be the plan."
> —JEFF BEZOS, FOUNDER AND CEO OF AMAZON

Indeed, my formative business-building years were a bit rocky. Thinking back to the early years, just after I'd launched my company, I remember all the business and entrepreneurial books I read that talked about the importance of writing great mission and vision statements. They always make me wonder where I would be today if I'd followed that advice.

This also leads me to ask: have you written yours yet? Or have you ever gone on weekend retreats with your top lieutenants in an attempt to clearly summarize your business among yourselves? Was it a productive use of one or more days?

I've been on many of these retreats over the years. I commonly refer to them—for the sake of my wife's better understanding—as "business trips." She had an especially hard time buying into this when I told her I had a "business trip" to Disney World and would be spending time in the parks for two days. I also eloquently called it "business relationship building," which is actually more accurate. I'm not sure it helped warm her to the concept.

One of my problems with mission statements and business planning retreats, or whatever you choose to call them, is all the great buzzwords that seem to fit into them. My favorite buzzword this month, for example, is "ecosystem." I'm not sure why I'd put that word into a mission statement, but I think it sounds very current and cool. It would fit. It also fits in nicely with the other words you so often see used in these statements, whether they actually apply to the business or not. These include "values," "character," "shareholder value," "culture," and "profitability."

These are all great words for use in a mission statement. They're also the reason why most mission statements sound so similar and rarely have much bearing on what actually happens with the philosophy of a business.

If you do currently have a mission or vision statement, try asking yourself and your employees this question: "Do you know what it says?" Without looking at it, can your employees repeat its key principals and values? Regardless of how much time you might have spent carefully crafting that statement, I'm willing to bet almost none of your employees could repeat it back to you. Few could even tell you, in their own words, what it means.

Most often, the catchy common phrases and words in these documents have little place in a planning document for a small business. This is because the small business planning bull's-eye actually requires a very different spin on conventional business planning from what you normally see in larger operations.

You Gotta Follow the Right Plan

Conventional business planning is usually mapped out in chunks of time—between two and five years. Small business planning generally must take into account the fact that you simply can't predict what will happen with the average small or very small business two years from now, let alone five. CEOs of SBs must be able to move and shift much faster to survive.

As an entrepreneur running a small company, "survival" is the one word that best summarized my formative years. It will for you, too. During your journey, you'll create your own stories—both good and bad. These events and how they were handled will develop the imprint of your business experience—regardless of what your plan might have suggested would happen.

When my first business was getting off the ground, I was very happy if I managed to plan for the next week. Often, I was delighted if I was at least able to plan for the next day. Small business is very fluid. Decisions are being made hourly, and new sales planning and decision-making happen constantly. It's hard, basically impossible, to predict the future of your small or very small company, as much as we all want to. Feel free to try, but I promise you, it'll change and take a different path. Hey, that's part of the fun of the journey. If you don't agree, running your own small company—and the pressures associated with it—may not be for you.

As I've mentioned many times now, small business is different from big business. Quite a bit different. Yes, we need to plan—at least for the short term. Yes, it's great advice to keep that plan in mind, revisit it, and adjust it often. Unlike their "big corporate" counterparts, however, business plans (if we can even use that word at the formative stages of your company) must be reviewed daily. If not daily—often. We can't go off on strategic retreats in far off-places and powwow to develop our long-term plans and end-game goals. Too much would change in our businesses during the short time we were gone!

Side Note: As a small business owner, most of my planning retreats took place in a twenty-four hour diner over an egg-white omelet as we discussed how we were going to make payroll for the coming week.

Death by Overplanning: It's Possible!

When it comes to small business planning, you can actually miss the target if you overplan by aiming too far out. It's common for business owners to plan for just several months out, as they agree upon the strategic direction for the company. So don't overplan, but do plan. As Benjamin Franklin said, "If you fail to plan, you are planning to fail."

When it comes to small or very small business, I prefer Nike's possibly more famous saying, "Just do it." I think this is great advice. Go out and make things happen. Simple things like picking up the phone or seeing a prospective customer. Make yourself feel vulnerable, and get out of your comfort zone. You'll feel alive. Do what must be done to keep pushing forward. That's how small business grows.

By comparison, a big business is more like a large ocean liner. It's tough turning those babies around quickly and a crew and careful planning is required to get the job done. A small business, by comparison, is more like a cigarette racing boat that can turn quickly and go really fast. This is precisely why the most effective planning in a small business is often short term and strategic. Then, maintain the fortitude to try new initiatives, even if they weren't in the original "plan."

I don't want you to think I'm demeaning vision statements, strategic planning, or strategic retreats. They certainly do have their place. I'm just saying they don't work well for small businesses the way they do for bigger businesses. Small business owners tend to do things by instinct. We tend to have a gut feeling when things are right. We might try a new ad campaign, run a promotion aimed at a specific demographic, or hire an employee without doing all the usual background checks.

Use whatever data you can personally obtain to make each decision, but realize there's also a fine line between micromanaging every aspect of your business and focusing on the bigger picture to keep growing your company. CEOs who "get" this will truly create something special.

Focus on the month-end performance against similar periods in the past. You should also track the cash going in and out. At the early stages of a business, this is far more strategically important—and more prone to change—than planning for the next five years would allow for.

We don't need to keep our eye out as far as the captain of that ocean liner—but we still have to keep track of how far we've come and how we got here to successfully reach our destination in the speedboat we've launched.

8:00 P.M.

Lots of Small Accounts or One Big Fish?

> "Easter is the only time of the year when it's
> perfectly safe to put all your eggs in one basket."
>
> —AUTHOR UNKNOWN

My mother is a smart woman. She once told me, "Nothing happens without sales." I know the statement is simplistic at its heart, so stop rolling your eyes. Still, you have to admit, that was some pretty savvy mom-talk there.

Side Note: To be honest, I'm not entirely certain if it was actually she who told me this, but I wanted to include my mom in the book, and this seemed like a great way to add her. The statement, itself, is true, whether my mom said it or not.

When it comes to creating a successful business, sales are what drives the company forward. Sales and the revenue it represents should always be at the top of the "to-do" list. Without dollars coming in, your business won't last long—unless you have a family trust fund that can finance all your ideas into the foreseeable future. Since most of us don't have one of those nice financial fallbacks, it's a good idea for the rest of us to focus on generating sales.

Schools of Thought . . . and Fish

There are two primary schools of thought about the development of an SB sales plan. One philosophy is to focus on a few large clients who each generate lots of revenue—by either placing large orders or by buying up a large portion of your available service time—at your highest rates.

Another approach is to work with many "small fish" in your revenue pond. Personally, I'm always aiming for the model that attracts many smaller business clients into my fold. This helps me avoid becoming dependent on one specific client.

The healthiest mix, of course, is to have a combination of both. Our company was fortunate to amass a healthy portfolio of small and medium-sized businesses into our credit card processing portfolio. We also had some Fortune 500 clients that added lots of credibility due to their name recognition, but not necessarily to our bottom line because of the ultra-thin margins.

As we developed our sales model for Charge Card Systems, our target market was the business owner with revenues ranging from $1 million to $25 million annually. Our merchants wanted a competitive financial solution with great service, and that's what we delivered.

There is no right or wrong answer for your ensuing plan. Different companies have different approaches. I do think the "big fish" approach brings with it far too many risks. If you lose even one of those "big fish," a significant portion of your business will swim away. When you have lots of small and mid-sized accounts, losing one of them won't send your business into a tailspin, if it has any impact at all.

As we grew our credit card business, one metric we studied monthly was our attrition numbers and the impact of those lost merchants to our bottom line. Losing one or two smaller accounts didn't significantly affect profitability, especially because we continued to add new merchant accounts monthly and continued to have thousands of merchants nationally. Even the impact of losing one of our Fortune 100 or 500 clients would have been dampened and easily overcome with the rest of the client business we still maintained.

Our approach made it a lot easier for me to sleep at night.

Marbles for Money

A friend of mine had a company that sold marble and stone products to neighborhood retail stores. His products were ultimately used for bathrooms, kitchens, and other home improvements. After years of approximately $2 million in sales per year, his company made a major breakthrough: the first purchase order from one of the larger big-box home stores in the country came in.

It seemed like a real coup. He'd finally gotten his foot in the door, and all his years of hard work would be rewarded with huge sales. It meant major revenues all at once from a single source. However, he also found that he started having less and less time available for his smaller accounts.

In the end, it nearly bankrupted him. The big-box store also wanted him to change everything about how he ran his company, insisting he change his accounting and delivery systems. Making all the required changes, of course, took time. It also cost money. It might not matter so much to a larger corporation with sophisticated systems and staffing to make changes, but, to a small business, all these fundamental changes in the way business is conducted can be a disaster.

Big companies, for example, aren't interested in prepaying for orders. Instead, they have the leverage to push their suppliers onto their payment schedule. This often leads to lengthy delays—as long as 100 days—before the SB owner receives payment. Meanwhile, the SB CEO still has to pay overhead and production costs, as well as deliver those goods, before the payment for them comes in.

I've too often witnessed many of my friends' companies failing—along with far too many other businesses—and filing bankruptcy or simply closing their doors. Many times, it's because they fell into the "one big fish" syndrome. They focused on that big client at the expense of the still very valuable smaller clients they had in their stable, or who were waiting to jump in from the sidelines.

It feels fantastic when you land a big fish client or customer. The immediate income bump is certainly nice. It's also nice not having to constantly chase down a bunch of smaller clients looking for payments. One big check arrives from your whale after you send that invoice their way and wait the amount of time they demand you wait before payment is issued. Life seems wonderful.

That's all well and good. But I just described the upside of "one big fish" syndrome. It can feel wonderful—until the day your prized "big fish" gets lured into another net, decides to change how they do business (no longer requiring your services), or enters an entirely different business where your help isn't needed. This is when those checks suddenly stop and you're not sure anymore how you'll manage to pay the bills or make payroll.

I'd really rather not see you wind up there.

9:00 P.M.

Residual Income—The Holy Grail for Any Business

> "If you understood residual income, you
> would walk through a brick wall to get it."
>
> —ART JONAK, ENTREPRENEUR AND
> NETWORK MARKETER

As our merchant processing business grew, I was totally amazed by the exponential value of adding just $100 additional per month in recurring revenue to our credit card processing income stream. I'd sit down monthly with all of our salespeople to explain the power of residual growth and how the rewards accumulate in return for some hard, dedicated work now.

To help better explain the explosive power of earning residual income, let's review the math involved in the credit card processing industry. This is analogous to other industries with a similar business model.

To keep the mathematics simple, let's assume that each

account will generate $100 a month in profit and that a full-time salesperson should be able to close ten deals per month. Of course, some deals would be less profitable and others could be thousands per month, but the average for this example is $100. That means, in a thirty-day month, our people could and should write one deal every three days (people shop on weekends, so our salespeople were always interacting with potential store owners, retailers, and restaurant owners).

At the end of just one year, a salesperson who followed this formula would sell 120 deals at $100 monthly each. Using the power of residual income, sales from that activity would equal:

Month 1 = $1,200	Month 7 = $8,400
Month 2 = $2,400	Month 8 = $9,600
Month 3 = $3,600	Month 9 = $10,800
Month 4 = $4,800	Month 10 = $12,000
Month 5 = $6,000	Month 11 = $13,200
Month 6 = $7,200	Month 12 = $14,400

The total for year one of gross monthly revenue would be $93,600. Using month twelve as an indicator—and even if that salesperson sold nothing the following year and no clients left our service—their existing clients would generate ongoing gross revenue of $172,800.

Clearly the benefits of a residual business model like this can be significant. I realize some businesses don't have a recurring revenue model they can follow. If there's no way to add a recurring revenue stream, maintain a solid focus on keeping every client you attract as happy as possible. This will help generate ongoing revenue from repeat sales. In many ways, the results, while maybe not as spectacular as they can be with residual revenue, will be similar.

I hope my example demonstrates how ongoing revenues on this scale can help a company earn real "power money"—for your salespeople and for the organization.

Using this business model, these accounts are running in the background, generating steady income over the ensuing years. Their maintenance is minimal in the case of the credit card processing industry—so low the salesperson has plenty of time to spend cultivating another 120 new accounts that will begin generating even more income for the next year.

This is the power of growing residual income. Generating repeat sales from existing relationships is easy to do when your company has dedicated salespeople on board who understand this concept. It generates excellent, reliable, ongoing income for the company and a steady income for the salesperson.

It's important to note that residual income also provides excellent insulation from even the most prolonged of financial downturns in the economy. Clients who are paying smaller monthly fees are also far more likely to stay on board even when times are leaner. If a few of them do elect to leave, the sting isn't nearly as detrimental to your bottom line, because there are still so many more who stay.

Recurring revenue is also anticipated revenue, especially if it's contracted and coming from a large number of clients. The assumption of having a set number of dollars that you know will be hitting the bottom line every month makes budgeting more comfortable. It also makes it far easier to obtain bank financing because anticipated income is also seen by lenders as an asset. A proven business model with solid reliable revenue growth demonstrates that the business will have the ability to repay bank loans. You might never need a bank loan, but there are many times when conventional bank or other forms of small business financing can help an SB grow.

Transactional versus Residual

As I said before, it was only after I had become involved in the payments industry that I fully understood the value of "residual" or "recurring" income.

Prior to the payments industry, I was in the promotional and advertising specialty industry. Our company earned our money by selling 500 pens,1,000 umbrellas, 100 T-shirts, and a myriad of other products to corporations for use as advertising pieces to promote their brands.

After completion of a promotional products order, we had to continuously nurture the relationships with our clients to hopefully receive future orders for other products. That's how you build and grow a transaction-based business.

The concept of a solid arsenal of residual sales coming in regularly is that you'll continue to make money in the future with very little additional effort—at least in theory.

Just look at the Netflix model, and you'll see everything I'm talking about in action on a huge scale. They charge millions of paying members somewhere around $9 a month. With multiple millions per month in bankable revenue, they negotiate deals for programming and create their own original shows for their members, pay their operating expenses, and generate growing profits.

Subscription services are clearly one of the best ways to enter into the residual market. This is why cable television and mobile phone service are such lucrative businesses.

I once read an interview with a business owner in England who makes significant subscription revenue selling—black socks. Yes. Men's black socks. It seems black socks were an important part of proper British business attire—at least, they were at the time the article was written. Please correct me if you live in England and this is incorrect or no longer true. Anyway, this fellow decided to start selling black socks online. His business made it easy for young British businessmen to order their required black socks online, at affordable prices, delivered directly to their doorsteps.

He had a tough go of it at first. He was making sales, but the business wasn't really growing. Then, he added an optional subscription service to his order forms. Businessmen in England would go through a lot of black socks, he reasoned. He figured they'd be more than willing to order a set number of pairs to be automatically sent to their doorstep every month. He called it his "Sockscription" service, and it became an ongoing revenue stream for his business that helped him turn a very simple online concept into millions of dollars.

Often, you can incorporate a subscription service or recurring revenue element into a transactional business if you give it some thought and truly understand the mindset of your customers. The Sockscription was created by a business originally set up to sell socks online, one pair at a time. That would probably have made some money, but it took off when the CEO added Sockscriptions to the menu.

Look for something about the products or services you sell that people would ordinarily buy regularly over time. Perhaps there are some added "perks" you could throw in for people who join your subscription service. This can usually be applied easily to anything people consume regularly—and to most services that people use on a repeat basis.

Even if your subscription service carries a small fee—let's say, between $10 and $20 per month—there's great money to be made. Provide your subscribers with genuine value, quality, and excellent service, and you'll grow. Just 5,000 to 10,000 customers paying $10 to $20 each can result in staggering monthly revenues your business can rely on.

As you consider launching your own entrepreneurial venture, I highly recommend looking at residual-based industries such as insurance, home alarms, gyms, health clubs, storage units, and—of course—the credit card industry. You'll be able to tap into some reliable ongoing revenue streams from a large number of small customers with these and similar businesses. You stand a great chance of maintaining profitably for the long haul, and your hard work today will pay financial dividends in the future.

That's why we do this.

The "Ins and Outs" of the Credit Card Processing Industry

> "Money is just the poor man's credit card."
>
> —MARSHALL MCLUHAN, CANADIAN PHILOSOPHER

I think it would be interesting to provide more information on the business I recently sold in 2012. I felt I'd uncovered a business holy grail when I first discovered the residual income possibilities from my entrée into the credit card processing industry. As the former cofounder of Charge Card Systems, the credit card processing company in which I spent much of my adult working life, I believe I'm obliged to include a chapter about my industry—if nothing else, so my children and grandchildren can one day read about what I actually did to make a living.

Lots of businesses accept credit cards as a form of payment, so I'm going to provide basic information about Visa, MasterCard, and American Express that the majority of business owners don't understand. If you're not interested in learning about merchant services, first I ask you, "Why not?" If you have a good answer for that question and you're ready to move the clock ahead to 11:00 p.m., go ahead! I won't be hurt.

I promise that my information in this chapter will save you a minimum of four times the price you paid for the book! If you don't feel you've received this value, just call or email me, and I'll be happy to refund your money (you'll just need to return the book).

The chances are very good your business will accept Visa, MasterCard, Discover, and American Express. Whether your company is a start-up or an existing business, you must meet the needs of your clients and customers. Credit and debit cards, gift and loyalty cards, and all forms of electronic payment processing are growing exponentially worldwide. Consumers also carry less cash. Electronic payments are on the rise as a result—especially with the emergence of Apple Pay and other processing technologies.

Today, even merchants who only sell products from a rented table at the flea market on weekends can quickly and easily process credit card and electronic check transactions with customers.

Your iPhone and Android have now replaced the traditional wallet. They're rapidly replacing the cash register, too.

Did you know that electronic payments are literally taking over point-of-sale purchases? According to market research released May 12, 2014, from Javenlin Strategy & Research, only 23 percent of all point-of-sale purchases are expected to be made with cash by 2017. That means credit card acceptance, by 2017, will be roughly 75 percent of all sales made in stores!

For this reason, it's definitely time for our discussion "Credit Card Processing 101." I feel it's important—right here, right now—for me to introduce you to the inner workings of how the credit card processing industry operates. Don't worry—it's just an overview. After all, I want to help you avoid drudgery, not subject you to it.

Unless your business already has a merchant account, you will have to consider a lot of variables when you first establish one. Even if your business already has an existing merchant account, I strongly suggest you continue reading. I'm positive that I can save you hundreds, if not thousands, of dollars each year by providing insider scoop and tips for significantly reducing your processing fees. This will increase your profitability.

There are also tricks that can enable you to receive your money the next day, unlike many processors who deposit your funds into the bank two to four days after you run the charges. Cash flow is king, and it's always better to have your money in your bank account than to have Visa and MasterCard and the acquiring banks hold your money.

To start, there are three basic types of merchant accounts. Your business will be classified within one of these three categories:

1. Retail or swiped merchant account

2. Mail order/telephone order account

3. Internet business

The first scenario includes retailers, restaurants, and other businesses where the customer physically presents his or her credit card to the merchant for payment. The second scenario is for merchants and companies that receive payments via telephone or direct mail. You send them your credit card number in the mail or provide it on the phone as your payment. The third scenario includes all online businesses. This last category is growing rapidly, as customers have become more comfortable paying for products and services on the web and online sales continue to grow year after year.

Within the payments industry, merchants are either considered "conventional merchants" or classified as "high risk." High risk is an entirely different classification due to numerous factors. While founding Charge Card Systems, my partners and I also started a company called Alternative Merchant Processing, which specializes in working with high-risk merchant types.

Uncover the Hidden Fees

There are also a number of hidden fees in the credit card industry that can unnecessarily inflate the overall cost of your processing bill. In reality, most businesses are woefully unaware of the pitfalls these fees can present—or how much they can adversely affect your bottom line.

Visa, MasterCard, and Discover maintain different rate structures for different types of cards, based on how the transaction is processed and what type of card is being accepted by the merchant. For example, there's a higher fee structure for transactions that are entered manually. These transactions are generally taken over the phone or by mail or fax and then entered into the terminal by the merchant by hand without the actual card being swiped through a physical credit card terminal. Non-swiped transactions increase potential liability and raise a flag because of possible fraud, as the actual card being used isn't presented physically to the merchant.

American Express is set up differently. It has a flat percentage fee based on the industry type they've assigned to your business, plus a transaction fee.

To highlight the differences in pricing, a business that's set up to mainly swipe cards in person—a dry cleaner, for example—may be charged as little as 1.79 percent of the amount of each transaction. There are still other fees that will make the 1.79 percent go higher. These can sneak this amount up to as high as 3.60 percent, depending on numerous factors, including whether the card accepted is a personal credit, debit, rewards, international, or corporate card. Did you know that you, as a business owner, pay more in fees to accept a corporate card? Crazy!

Reading and understanding your merchant agreement is vital to make sure you do everything possible to keep your rate at its lowest. It makes sense, right?

In addition to discount rates (what we in the industry call the percentage of each transaction that we charge merchants for our services), there are also transaction fees to consider.

Less Could Be More

Some credit card processing companies will offer "no" transaction fees. It's important to understand, however, that not having a transaction fee doesn't necessarily mean you're getting the best overall rate structure, in spite of how companies might try to portray it.

Many processing companies play "games" and "lie" about how low your rates will be should you sign up with their company. Many firms offer a low introductory discount rate. Companies will often bundle their rate and combine the discount rate and the transaction fee to attract new business. This provides the illusion of a better rate structure. Be aware that this isn't necessarily a better deal—or even a reasonable one.

It's My Money, and I Want It Now

Two issues to understand when choosing your processing company: the funding of the merchant's account after processing, and the collection of the fees involved. Do you know how long it takes from the time you settle a new batch of credit card charges (usually every day), until your money is deposited safely into your bank account? If you don't know, make it a point to check.

Will it take twenty-four, forty-eight, or seventy-two hours for your money to hit the bank? You want to verify this because, for some industry types, funding can take as long as a week. Guaranteed twenty-four hour funding is available in the industry. Ask for it.

Let's face it. It's always tempting, considering the costs and/or complexity involved with credit card processing, to try to work around it or to skip it altogether. But it's close to impossible to run a business that doesn't accept payment by credit card these days, as much as you might think you'd like to try.

I guarantee you—many companies don't want to pay the so-called 2 percent fee charged to accept credit cards (everyone always assumes its 2 percent, for some reason). But they also understand business will be lost if they fail to make this convenient payment method available. This will have much more impact on their bottom line than the fees ever could.

Did They Just Say I Was High Risk?

Take a breath. Relax. No one's slamming you if this is your classification. High risk doesn't mean you're being accused of running drugs or taking bets in the back room. You're not personally being labeled risky. But your business may have risk parameters that move it from classification as a "traditional" merchant to a high risk. Rather than questioning the integrity of your business, this nomination, instead, could also mean that the market you're serving has been deemed high risk for various reasons.

Some industries that fall into the high-risk category include:

○ Adult industry websites (no surprise)

○ Travel and vacation clubs

○ Debt collection

○ Electronic cigarettes

○ Memberships

○ Subscriptions

○ Herbal supplements

○ Online pharmacies

○ Ammunition stores

○ Medical discount plans

○ Many, many more

Business owners with poor credit will also fall into the high-risk category. Businesses with excessive charge-backs on their credit card transaction history are also deemed to be more risky than a traditional business type.

It Gets Better: Auto-Revenue and More for Less

Today's modern credit card merchant processing enables automatic recurring revenue to be possible.

I don't think I could readily recommend that you chase after small amounts of small recurring revenue from lots of customers if you had to manage thousands of clients on your accounts receivable ledger to pull it off. Fortunately, automatic billing on your customer's credit card is an extremely simple program that can be set up with the click of a mouse and automates the entire processes to make your life much easier. We live in wonderful times!

Accepting debit and credit cards is critical in today's business environment. The fees associated with accepting these cards is a cost of doing business. I hope the information I've divulged will enable you to better understand your fees and the importance of minimizing them as you grow your company. Budget them into your financial planning. Offering credit cards will definitely attract more customers and increase the size of your average transaction versus just accepting cash.

Do your due diligence. Get the best deal on processing you can.

Let's Waste Some Money!

"Risk more than others think is safe.
Dream more than others think is practical."

—HOWARD SCHULTZ, CHAIRMAN AND CEO
OF STARBUCKS

Huh? Did I really just suggest you waste money? Isn't this about the most counterintuitive thing you've ever heard . . . especially in a book about small business, startups, and trying to make money?

Despite what you might think, I have a theory that, in business, it's sometimes a good idea to "waste" some money if you want to experience serious growth. It might surprise you even more to know that I think this is especially important in a startup businesses that isn't yet cash-flow positive.

I know. It sounds crazy. But hear me out. When I lay out my budgeting process, it's fairly easy to quantify the main expense categories: they include the usual vital items—employees, marketing, and rent, for example. But I also always make sure I include a "waste money" line item. This "waste money" category is for funds reserved for doing something totally outside the box of conventional thinking. This was our risk-taking capital, earmarked to be spent in support of something that could (and most likely would) fail—as long as it was also a concept that had the potential to bring us excellent results if the idea took fire and worked out.

Depending on the size of your company, the number you put in this expense category will vary. The good news is that it's entirely up to you how much you decide to allocate to this portion of your budget. For example, when I started my first business, I allocated $10,000 to this category. This was while I was running a young start-up with little revenue and even less profit. As we grew into a more mature company, the amount in that account was closer to $100,000 annually.

Think of the "waste money" expense line as an investment fund!

Side Note: If you're getting into your own business or joining a business in a senior management role, you'll want to start using business language like I just did. "Invested" does sound much better than "lost," doesn't it? I also love using the word "capital" instead of "money." But that could just be me.

Back to the point—that fund also occasionally brought us a home run. But you don't have to just take my word for it. I'll tell you about two of them right now.

Win, Place, or Show

How did I choose to "waste" money profitably? Years ago, most credit card processing companies were only attending "end-user shows"—trade shows for restaurants and retailers. That's when my web developer said he'd heard about a national web developers show in Las Vegas.

I was intrigued by the possibilities of reaching outside the normal trade-show box for our industry. However, coming from New Jersey, staying for a three-day show—with the cost of travel, hotel, booth space, and two employees—was going to cost us in excess of $10,000. That's a significant amount of money for almost any start-up business (or any business for that matter), especially if not funded by private equity or venture capital firms.

Instead of being completely concerned over every dollar, I knew I had my "waste money" fund established with $10,000 in it. Having these outside-the-box funds available made the decision much easier to make. I'm certain I wouldn't have gone to that show if it meant pulling the funds from another part of our still-thin budget.

The $10,000 evaporated within those three days. I worked as hard as anyone possibly could, talking with every potential client I could identify at the show and making sure they all visited my luxuriously roomy booth. (Kidding aside, I barely had room to stand in front of my booth without bumping into the other exhibitors.) Still, I was frustrated by anyone who didn't want to politely look at my trifold brochures as they walked by. I also had a fish bowl to attract business cards, complete with a promotional offer for a cruise to the Caribbean, which I had hoped would incentivize prospective customers to visit my booth.

Following the conference, I continued working. I made my follow-up calls and sent out follow-up emails. And it worked! I established some great relationships from that one show. That $10,000 has exponentially grown, turning into hundreds of thousands of dollars in revenue over time.

The risk I took making this investment paid off. This time. Many times, "waste money" fund investments are a bust. Still, when I look back over my career and my use of that "waste money" fund, I know it's provided a positive return on my total investment.

Face to Face—Boom!

Another way I've used the "waste money" fund with good results is covering travel expenses to see potential prospects. In this day and age of technology with Skype meetings and video conferencing making life simple, it probably doesn't seem like there's really much reason to travel across the country to have a face-to-face meeting anymore.

Or is there?

I'd argue, instead, that building a personal relationship of trust with a prospective new client is paramount to my success, and this only really happens by looking a potential client or vendor in the eye, face to face—not virtually. Taking the easy technology-driven way out is . . . well . . . easy. But, when you can get out of the office and interact with people in person, so much more happens. The conversations are more engaging, as is the laughter and the dialogue. The relationship vibe strengthens and grows every minute you're engaged in this manner.

Get out and see people. It's still important today, and, with fewer and fewer people doing it, you'll stand out even more in the memories of every potential client you meet when you do. Your "waste money" fund is a great way to finance these meetings.

Oddball Wins Are Never Planned

I want you to understand that it's important, if at all possible, to keep some money on hold—just for the oddball opportunities that will pop up along the way in business from time to time. There's going to be a moment when you feel in your bones that an opportunity—one that seems totally unrelated to whatever it is you ordinarily do—is actually a perfect fit. If you don't have at least some money you can waste without worrying about seeing a return, you can't give it a try. You might not, for example, attend a trade show or fly to meet an important potential client, one on one.

Since developing the concept of this "waste money" fund, I'm surprised by how few people I talk to ever considered having one. Most wouldn't think twice about putting money away for the occasional emergencies and unexpected expenses that crop up when launching a new business. Almost no one ever seems to think of also putting some money back to use on ideas and opportunities that might at first appear wild on the surface, but also just might kick back an ROI of many times what you spent.

You want to always make certain you're in a position to take advantage of unpredictable, possibly risky opportunities when they show up and make sense. These funds make it possible to truly think outside the box. That "waste money" fund is the key to that box—the key that can let you out—where potentially huge hidden profits reside.

Whatever you do, keep pushing the envelope. Look for new opportunities. Don't worry if your latest idea sounds crazy or feels like a money-waster. Stay within your "waste money" fund, but don't be afraid to throw some of these funds at an idea if there's a reasonable chance it could work well.

You could look at putting money into this fund as kind of like another form of insurance, if it makes it easier. Call it "unexpected opportunity insurance," get it funded, and get rolling.

In the words of a famous maker of athletic products: "Just do it"—to which I'd like to add, "And never look back."

Golf: It's a Lot More Than Whacking Some White Balls Around

> "Golf and sex are about the only things you can enjoy without being good at."
>
> —JIMMY DEMARET, AMERICAN PROFESSIONAL GOLFER

Another great example for some of that "waste money" fund is spending money to learn to play golf—and your time is golf. I could probably write an entire book about golf. Maybe I will! But for now, I'll just write a chapter on this subject.

For now, I want you to know that I love the sport and I'm pretty good at it, but I could always be better. I have my Saturday game with my friends; however, one of my favorite reasons to play golf is networking with other people in the business world. It can lead to some very interesting insights. It allows me to connect with people I didn't consider contacts before we played and turned them into contacts after making the rounds.

It's also a lot more fun meeting people on the links than it is meeting them in restaurants, office buildings, or networking functions. And—wow—you can learn a lot about someone after four hours on the links together . . . the good, the bad, and the ugly.

Of course, this could also be your downfall—unless you make your living as a pro golfer. It's up to you to determine whether playing golf is the best use of four to five hours of your time. Just remember—as they say in the lottery—play wisely!

There are successful executives who believe you have no future in business if you don't play golf. I don't subscribe to that theory, but you'd better replace golfing with involvement in something: fishing, networking groups, or other hobbies where you can interact with people on a level that's not directly related to your work.

Seriously, some of the most successful entrepreneurs I know have mastered the fine art of building business relationships and even closing deals during a game of golf. The golf experience itself always creates a permanent bond—whether you're playing with friends, family, or business associates. It naturally builds relationships that are then carried through life. This explains why so many successful entrepreneurs have closed literally thousands of deals and nurtured special and long-lasting relationships on the golf course. I want you to do this, too. Think about it.

The Right Way to Play

Here are some tips I've picked up from my own networking on the greens:

Spend your time on the course building relationships. Have

fun. Forget trying to be "on." Don't try to sell anything. You wouldn't go into a new networking group and immediately try closing deals on your first day. Don't do it on the golf course, either. If all you want to do is "talk shop" while you play, you run the risk of annoying the other golfers. This will result in a bad day of golfing for them, if not for you. There's no way that a bad day of golf will increase your chances for closing a deal—so focus on the golf, the fun, and the friendships that are formed before those relationships have been solidified.

First and foremost, invest in people—not projects or ideas. Use your time playing golf to demonstrate that you're smart, competent, and likeable. Show the other players that you're a thoughtful golfer. Engage in quality conversation, and you'll wind up a lot more likely to close deals when the time is right.

To expand your network, go to the course alone. This gets you placed into a foursome with strangers. There's plenty of time to engage in conversations and get to know everyone in your foursome during eighteen holes—and you'll form a bond with everyone in a way you can't possibly accomplish online or over the phone.

I already told you to avoid jumping right into business topics. As you progress through your round, however, start asking questions that will entice the other parties to share more information about their own businesses or what they do for a living. Give them the courtesy of really listening. Pay careful attention to any specific problems or bottlenecks you hear them talking about that you might be able to help them with. Introduce them to someone who might solve the problem or point them to some specific information that could help. This will come back to you many times over.

Always bring some business cards with you to the game. Exchange them with the other folks in your foursome before you end the round, and then schedule a lunch or, at least, connect with them on LinkedIn following the game.

Whatever you do, don't cheat. As much fun as golf can be, winning isn't the object here and cheating for a lower score will only hurt your chances to get any other connection going with your foursome. Yeah. I've seen this firsthand. It isn't pretty.

Always arrive on time. This is especially important when you've invited potential clients or suppliers to join you for a game. Keeping them waiting starts everything off with the wrong impression. You might as well just stay in the office if you don't follow this rule.

Leave your competitive nature at the office. Remind yourself that you're playing golf to build a rapport. Building that rapport successfully is the "win" you're going after. Again, winning the match on the eighteenth hole isn't the objective here, regardless of how much winning might matter to you otherwise.

Should you wager on the game? At this level of play, it's expected. It also helps build rapport by making the game itself more fun. Just keep the betting friendly—meaning keep the stakes low. I recommend the Nassau side bet, which is three bets for the round—$2 each—on the low score on the front and back nine and on the full eighteen-hole round.

No excuses! It doesn't matter if you're a new player hitting the links with seasoned golfers—just tell them you're new and open to any tips or suggestions they might have for improving your game so you move things along quickly. They'll appreciate your honesty, teach you something along the way, and like you better in the end. Even if you lose.

Size Doesn't Matter

Watch your anger. Maybe your bad day on the links is just that—a surprisingly bad day. They happen. Don't curse, throw your clubs, or stomp around. Again, I've seen this in action, and it's never a pretty thing to behold.

Compliment everyone you're playing with on any good shots and putts. Be sincere . . . don't fake it.

Consider getting some golf balls with your company logo on them. You knew I'd think of this one, right? Seriously, provide some to your foursome before tee time. This really works.

If you're familiar with the course, give the other players the benefit of your experience and share some tips for what to watch out for as you play each hole. Everyone you're playing with will appreciate and remember you.

Plan the outing to include lunch or a nineteenth hole get-together to get to know everyone better—and them you—even before the relationship gets started in earnest on the links.

Give the other golfers a chance to see the best you can be. Golf is a great way to make connections and form new relationships, but it's also one of the most revealing activities you can engage in when it comes to personality. When it comes to the good, the bad, and the ugly, don't show them anything but the good.

Watch the alcohol consumption. This is something that can undo everything you're trying to accomplish, if you fail to pay attention to this tip. If it's hot and you're drinking, it can be a total surprise how quickly you find you're drunk—and drunk people can very easily say or do the wrong thing. This is not what you're playing golf to accomplish. Swap out cold water with a beer or two, if you're drinking. If the other players aren't drinking . . . don't drink. Period. I've seen this one happen far too often, and it makes all the other no-no's I've described here look pretty in comparison when it does.

Treat everyone in the game like royalty. Sometimes, you'll run into someone who makes this very hard. Stay cool and treat them the same way anyway. The other players will see how you handle this type of person and appreciate you for it even more.

Do your homework when it comes to the course you choose. You want it to be one you'll all enjoy, so check to see if the course has just been aerated or if there is major construction going on at the facility, for example. These would not be good choices.

Don't choose the tees you play from. Remember, your goal is to provide potential clients and new relationships with a great experience getting to know you better. Play at their level, whatever that might be.

Be a good "golf course citizen." Repair divots on the course and ball marks on the greens, and rake any bunkers that need it. When someone else is playing a shot, stand away from them and out of their line of sight. Do I need to say it? Also be quiet during other people's swings. These simple actions, as basic as they might seem, will show your fellow players you're a person who respects the course and the other people playing on it . . . a great impression to leave anytime.

Just remember, the end result you're shooting for is a good, fun golf outing. Focus on the fun the other players are having, and you'll come away leaving a great impression. It's also a great opportunity to pick up some new business for many years to come.

It doesn't get a lot better than that.

If It's Good Enough for Alice . . .

If you still think all the hoopla surrounding golf is just a bunch of fanatics making excuses for getting on the links . . . consider this: One story I remember reading years back in my golf magazine involved seventies rocker Alice Cooper. It turns out he's a golf fanatic. He named a "tell-all" book he wrote about his life and career *Golf Monster* and plays the game often in celebrity tournaments. He's damn good, too.

Who knew, right?

How did he find his way from the stage into the sport? He said he discovered golf while he was in rehab, and he credits the game with saving his life. In his book, Cooper said golf gave him something healthier to focus his addictive nature on than drugs and booze. The rehab he was in had a great course, and he had little else to do while he was there . . . so he poured himself into the game.

Now he hobnobs with celebrities at tournaments, playing the finest golf courses in the world. One of his new life goals, in fact, is to play all the greatest golf courses in the world. It's his new "bucket list."

Do you think he does some networking while he plays? I'm certain of it. Despite what you might think of this aging rocker, the guy still keeps busy hosting a nightly syndicated radio show, making guest appearances on TV, and . . . yes . . . touring once in a while. These things require connections, and I'm betting ole Alice makes a lot of them as he plays.

Golf, then, is a lot more than just whacking little white balls around a giant yard with holes in it. It's a time to be outside in the fresh air with old friends and meeting new friends. I absolutely love it—even when I'm not playing so well, which is often. It's a pure sport.

I had the honor of playing Augusta National (the home of the Masters) several years ago. With the exception of my wedding day and the birth of my children, that may have been my most amazing day ever.

Side Note: I had to write the above paragraph to avoid the risk of a divorce! You know what I mean. Read between the lines. And, while we're here in this "side note," I'd be remiss if I didn't mention my daughter, Jennifer. She became a very good high school golfer and even shot thirty-nine in a high school tournament—her first and only time breaking forty for nine holes in competitive golf. I relish my memories of teaching her the game, visiting the driving range, and playing golf together on weekends throughout the years. And, in order that all my children love me equally, I would be remiss if I didn't mention Lexi, my tennis player, and Andrew, my basketball and lacrosse athlete. My times with my children on and off the fields are, and continue to be, very special for me. I absolutely love our time together! But enough about them for now. It's time to get back to the business portion of our program.

Selling Your Business— Or Time to Become an Employee . . . Again?

Entrepreneurs often state that their goal—their "ultimate end game"—is to eventually sell their business and cash out. It's their realization of the dream. They see it as the reaping of the rewards of their many years of long days and nights starting the business themselves or joining a start-up team and building it from the ground up.

I know I do tend to go on about building a "job" versus building a business, but I think it's a very important and vital distinction to keep clear. If you don't understand the differences and keep them front and center at all times, your chances of failure will go up exponentially.

Fortunately, it's easy to tell the difference. If you can picture your business running and still doing fine without you at the helm, then, congratulations, you've built a business. If the whole thing would fall apart without you, you've managed to build a job for yourself. It couldn't be much clearer than that.

The latter option can be a good thing if your nature is to always be in charge. There's nothing wrong with building a job for yourself, especially when it's your business. This will still provide you with a lot more potential and freedom than working at a job for someone else would ever likely provide. It will also give you a chance to do what you like in a way that working for someone else can't ever enable you to do.

For me, building a business that doesn't require my constant attention or much of my physical presence to continue profitably enables me to attain my vision of real freedom. There's also a solid sense of accomplishment knowing it was me who put in all the hours of sweat equity and struggle to get the business up and running.

How you do it is your choice. I'm not here to judge you either way.

Moving Toward the End Goal

The business I built with my partners matured over time. Tony and my dad were eventually able to work fewer hours. I even took a two-week vacation each of the past few summers—the first in my professional life, with the exception of my honeymoon (if you don't count the fact that I was never fully disconnected and constantly checked in on emails and client phone calls).

Yeah, I've definitely got the "bug." Bad.

If Tony and my dad had been employees, they wouldn't have lasted long. However, by building the company, putting in the time and effort to get it started, and then bringing it to where it was, they'd earned the right to do as they pleased. They'd both had very successful careers, and it was my turn to put in the long hours working on growing the business after their initial contributions were in place.

Of course, we could have still chosen to work more hours. We were, however—in our lives and in the business—at a place where finding balance in our lives between work, family, sports, and our other avocations was always kept in focus.

Creating a job for yourself is certainly fine, but ask yourself: what job could you get—or even build for yourself—that you can then hand off to your kids, providing them with a future?

We had built a business.

We were at that enviable point where the guidance and oversight of my partners backing my day-to-day involvement was all that was required to continue growing.

Then, in 2010, we started getting serious inquiries about selling the business. After numerous meetings with potential suitors, we agreed to sell to Card Connect, a well-established credit card company that was growing organically and ramping up that growth through acquisitions. Our deal allowed me to continue as president of the Charge Card Systems Division, with a three-year contract. The parent company terminated many of the redundant positions in our company due to duplication at their corporate offices.

I was always a very hard worker because I was raised with a great work ethic and an appreciation for a dollar. Our negotiations with Card Connect were fair and businesslike, and a genuine friendship evolved as we spent time together over the many months.

In the end, the deal closed, money was wired into our accounts, and we were all rewarded for the years of hard work and risks we'd taken building our company into an attractive target for acquisition.

Living in Surreality

It was a surreal feeling when we finally closed our transaction. Yes, I was staying on as the transitional president of our division of the company, but it was no longer my company. I was now—*gasp!*—an employee . . . and I hadn't been one or even used the word since my first job at Lehman Brothers.

It was strange being an employee again. In my mind, I knew I was still president, but my autonomy was gone. If I wanted to spend money on something I thought the company needed, I had to check with senior management and wait around for them to say yay or nay. The people at Card Connect are terrific, and I love working with them, but after years of making my own decisions, I found it felt truly odd asking for that permission.

It definitely took some getting used to.

I was still an owner with stock in the parent company. This was part of the terms and conditions of the sale, so I would continue to have a truly vested interest in the outcome of business— plus a salary and an upside, based on performance. Still, not being the person who has the last word felt . . . uncomfortably restrictive.

It's hard to describe the feeling until you experience it yourself.

Losing the Fire

There was something else I had to get used to after we sold the business: I started receiving a regular salary for the first time in many years. Money's all relative, and my salary wasn't enormous, but it was greatly appreciated. I'd not had a guaranteed regular salary since I was twenty-four years old.

For a lot of small business owners, it's that desire to make the next $100, then increase it to $1,000, and then to $100,000, that keeps them focused. If there's a guaranteed paycheck every week, even if it's small, it becomes harder and harder to feel the drive to hit certain monetary goals.

With many entrepreneurs I've spoken with, it's the hunt that keeps them going—the need to find the next great deal that keeps them excited. I was definitely one of them. I quickly discovered a salary made me lazy. It took away my drive to find more customers or to come up with the next possibly great idea. I suppose it was because I knew the check would come, either way—and I knew how big that check would be each time. To me, it was a lot like living in a birdcage when I was born with wings and needed to fly.

Which Are Thee—Employer or Employee?

The words sound very similar. They're almost spelled the same, too. Still, even though only an *r* and that final *e* separate the two, the definitions and connotations of "employer" and "employee" are exponentially different.

Within our company, there were only three equity participants who shared in the financial rewards of all the business transactions. We were the founders and earned the right by burning the midnight oil and putting in the very best of our talent and expertise to grow the business into a profitable entity. We didn't do it for a salary; it was our nature, our makeup, to work hard and one day potentially cash out (but this was not our driving force with the launch of our company).

We understood that putting in lots of hours and work in the beginning can, for the owners of a company, pay off with potentially huge profits and fewer hours of work and labor down the road. We saw the "big picture" and were willing to put a lot of other things aside to get it.

Employees came and went in our business. The differences between them and the founding team were clear. Employees are interested in what they can get—right now—in return for their time and effort today. They can't envision putting in hours away from home working on something that might pay them later—even if the payment at that time will be potentially gigantic.

Employees often feel a sense of pride when they're part of building a successful business—but they're part of a larger group of people sharing the success. The owners are the ones who feel the deep sense of satisfaction, in addition to pride, when it all takes off and starts working well.

So, which are you—employer or employee? You need to ask. Get inside yourself and see for sure which fits you best. You can still start and build a successful business either way, but this bit of introspection will help determine whether you start a business that's a job for you or one you can eventually step away from and sell or pass along to your heirs.

The Changing Face
of Money

"We teach children to save their money. As an attempt to counteract thoughtless and selfish expenditure, that has value. But it is not positive; it does not lead the child into the safe and useful avenues of self-expression or self-expenditure. To teach a child to invest and use is better than to teach him to save."

—HENRY FORD, FOUNDER OF FORD MOTOR COMPANY

Throughout the past decade of my involvement in the payments industry, I find everyone constantly talking about "money" in one way or another. I think about money in a different context when at home and how I want to raise my children to value and appreciate money.

With a lot of airplane travel, I had the time to write notes to help me when I had a planned in-depth conversation with my three children about the value and meaning of money. At the time, they were fifteen, thirteen, and eight years old. I wanted them to understand money in very basic terms and to see the evolution of money, and especially, how much it's changed since my childhood.

When I was a child, I vividly remember my piggybank. It was shaped like a basketball player, and it held all of my pennies, nickels, and quarters. Every few months, I'd wrap the coins in special paper tubes to bring to the bank and trade them in for a five-dollar bill—if I was lucky.

I remember, years later, calling my parents "collect" several times when I had no money to make a call from a payphone. It was always an enormous relief when I heard them tell the operator, "Yes—we'll accept the call." When was the last time you used a payphone? Just think of the changes that have taken place just as the result of cell phone technology! At what age did your children get their first cell phone? As adults, how "naked" do we all feel if we forget our cell phones, as if we've been suddenly disconnected from the world?

I remember my wife saying to me twenty years ago, "Do you have money in your wallet?" Now, the first question we always ask is, "Do you have your credit card with you?"

There are some people who still carry more than just a few dollars in cash in their wallets. I think it's more the exception than the rule nowadays. Do you use your credit card, debit card, prepaid card, stored value card, or gift card—instead of cash?

I think you get the idea.

Given the Lehman Brothers collapse, the Madoff horror, the banking crisis, and the mortgage industry meltdown, do we ever really think about the safety of our money sitting in our local bank? Will it be there for our future needs? Do you really understand what it means when your money is FDIC insured?

My notes continued:

An old cliché about money proclaims, "Money doesn't buy happiness." What do you think? I'd rather have it than not—but money doesn't define me. Of course, I want enough money to afford the things that are important in my life—shelter, food, college tuition, charity—and I certainly don't think I'd be human if I didn't also want a few luxuries, such as vacations. But is money, itself, a scorecard of your success? Do you think your life would really change if you made a lot more money? Would you live a different lifestyle? Would you buy more things?

Would you be happier?

Why do so many celebrities and famous people who made millions and are considered "rich" go broke and find themselves in total debt? Don't they understand the value of money and how it should be managed?

We hear about the cashless society and that it's eventually going to define our future. Perhaps it's already here with mobile payments, Google Wallet, PayPal, and so many other payment systems at our disposal. Many other technologies also affirm that we, as a population, will no longer be carrying a physical wallet in the years to come.

I hope these few thoughts might spark some additional thoughts for you about money and how you feel about it. It's truly amazing how, in just a few short years, money and our industry overall have both changed so much.

Big Data: It's Not Just for the Big Boys Anymore

> "Anything that is measured and
> watched, improves."
>
> —BOB PARSONS, FOUNDER OF GODADDY

Since the sale of Charge Card Systems, I've become involved as a consultant with a company called Affinity Solutions. The company's product is called Navigator. It helps a myriad of businesses from different industry types and companies of all sizes to track and measure the metrics from their marketing efforts and enables senior management to base future marketing by employing real data.

I believe in data . . . but it's always been too expensive or difficult to get the kind of data an SB really needs to succeed. Until now.

In a recent report from the Economist Intelligence Unit entitled "Big Data: Harnessing a Game-Changing Asset," several findings included:

- Over the last year, 73 percent of survey respondents said their collection of data has increased "somewhat" or "significantly."

- Companies that self-identified as "strategic data managers" tended to financially outperform their competition more than other.

- More than half of the companies surveyed reported that they expected the increased volume of data to improve operations, increase operational efficiency, inform strategic directions, improve customer service by understanding key drivers, and identify and develop new products and services.

The world of big data is clearly here now. It's also now ready for the small- to mid-size merchant who traditionally hasn't been exposed to this new kind of capability. This means that every organization now has an opportunity to leverage big data to its advantage—to drive accurate and timely decisions that can materially affect business and organizational goals. When you combine big data with big analytics, you quickly realize it presents an opportunity for every organization.

As John Wanamaker so eloquently stated in the early 1900s, "Half the money I spend on advertising is wasted; the trouble is, I don't know which half."

I've said it before. As a small business owner—especially one with years of experience—I do a lot of things by instinct. I, as well as many others like me, have gut feelings that often lead to the right decisions. Sometimes, that instinct's right on target. Other times—like the incident with my jailed bookkeeper—not enough background checking was done. I relied too much on that same instinct. It was a rare incident when the "gut test" failed me.

When it comes to many of the decisions business owners will face day to day, there are times when our instinct is the only device we have the resources (or, more often, the time) to turn to. Still, we don't want to rely on our intuition entirely, ignoring the power of testing, measuring, or analyzing a situation a bit before acting when the data is available.

Sometimes, it might seem too hard to try to understand all the statements and charts involved in running a business. It might even seem boring—a crushing blow to your creativity—going through everything required to fully investigate the various options you're considering. All that might be true. But, if you don't take the time to go through all the available data, seeking out all the answers, your business probably won't be around long.

The ability to perform data analytics and trend research, and then to build marketing campaigns derived from that data, are all gaining popularity and now being marketed aggressively within our industry. This valuable information provides you with the metrics needed for more informed decision-making to run your business, and to better understand your customers, based on the findings of concrete facts, in addition to the gut feeling by which we all tend to run.

Think of it as an affordable research "assist," and you'll see what I'm aiming at here.

Big data isn't just for big companies today—it's now attainable for all organizations of all sizes. This secure, scalable, and predictive data now provides even your SB with a management tool of enormous value.

This data helps businesses identify problems, recognize patterns, and gain meaningful insights. It enables you to answer such key questions as, "What ultimately drives sales?" "Which deals are most likely to close?" and "How do I make employees happy?"—or whatever it is you wish to know.

Whether you're the local neighborhood retailer or a large Fortune 500 company, you can now use this kind of data to better manage your business. Now, more than ever, entrepreneurs running SBs are also looking for these analytics—but, even more important, for information on how to use these numbers to provide actionable results.

You might have heard the phrase "analysis paralysis." Maybe you're hearing what I'm telling you, but still don't feel big data would be right for you because you're afraid it might be too much. That's not what I'm talking about here. You don't ever want to turn into one of those people who can't make a single move without waiting weeks for data and complete analysis of that data to show you the way. Instead, I'm talking about the opportunity to get solid insights that could mean the difference between closing a big deal and not closing it, and between developing a cost-effective marketing campaign that pulls in truly targeted leads and one that fails.

This new big data world isn't just about identifying problems faster. It's also about solving problems for which there weren't solutions before. When you put the right analytics to work on your big data problems, you can stop thinking of big data as some kind of challenge and start seeing it as the enormous opportunity for growth that it represents.

Take a look past the technical jargon, and you'll find that big data is about opportunity—the opportunity to learn from your company's existing data in order to make smarter business decisions. Larger companies have embraced big data for decades, but data analytics companies are now also embracing the SB marketplace with very robust programs.

As a small retailer, you can now use this type of data to analyze the relationship between social media conversations and buying trends to quickly capitalize on emerging sales opportunities. You can also understand how your pizza shop is doing right now (for example) relative to other pizza shops in your five or twenty-five mile radius, or when compared to other pizza parlors nationwide. Would it help to be able to see the category spend within a region, study competitive performance comparisons, identify trends over specific months as well as seasonality trends, then spell out detailed spending profiles, and determine the gross margin of your best-selling products? Or, perhaps, just to know which days of the week are most profitable for your industry as a whole?

What if, when launching a new online service, you were able to analyze your site's visitors and track how they move from page to page? Would it help to gain an understanding of what engages web visitors and the things that turn them off, and to detect promotional and cross-selling opportunities along that path?

I hope you get the point.

In the past, this kind of big data analytics project would have been far too costly and complex for a small business to take on. Some of the legacy analytics solutions on the market were initially built for larger enterprises—but this is all changing. The SB market is now ready for data analytics, and it's finally available at pricing that makes it affordable.

Hell, it's long overdue, if you ask me!

Data has clearly become more and more visible in all sizes

of businesses with the growth of the Internet, social media, and social networks. Ensuring up-to-date listings across relevant directories, directory updates, and continuous monitoring of the business's online reputation via top review sites is now critical to the livelihood of your enterprise.

It's essential, however, when you decide to start generating this kind of data for your business, that you choose a system that includes the following attributes:

1. Simplicity

A big data solution for small businesses should be easy to deploy. It should also use and require nominal time—not several months—and limited brain power to employ. SBs don't have lots of specialized personnel to start to analyze these programs. All the capabilities of the system should work together seamlessly, and it must run on the KISS principle—"Keep it simple, stupid."

In addition, the system shouldn't require staffers who have to undergo a lot of training. Instead, it should include self-service capabilities so that a broader audience of analysts and business users can make it run without the need for the IT department to become involved.

2. Cost

Data solutions for small businesses must be priced right. Data solutions have been available to SBs for a long, long time now—they just haven't been affordable until recently. CEOs should be able to pay only for the capabilities they need. The licensing strategy should allow them to start small and scale up as needed. This approach is particularly useful for a rapidly grow-ing small business, where it's critical to keep the cost and capa-bilities of software investments in alignment with the rate of growth and expansion of the operation. In some cases, this will establish a performance-based system where the merchant only pays based on success stories, rather than on a one-size-fits-all monthly fee.

3. Take Action

It's great to have all this solid information, but what do you do with it once you have it? As a small business owner myself, this is where the rubber meets the road. Information can be gener-ated to help provide intelligence for a myriad of purposes. The number-one thing a data gathering and analysis system should do for you is help you identify an actionable proactive response to take advantage of the numbers reported.

The service companies who deliver products in the data world also work with merchants and payment systems to extract and analyze proprietary data from credit card purchases. This infor-mation can then be used to measure sales performance, evalu-ate customers and customer segments, improve promotions and loyalty programs, launch more effective marketing campaigns, write better business plans, and perform other tasks that lead to smarter business decisions.

Although most big data discussions concern enterprises that have all the resources, such as data scientists and research firms, there are some ways your small business can gather, analyze, and make sense of data you most likely already have, if you know where to look.

Google Analytics

If you're ready to dive in and see what some solid data analytics can do for you, you can get started right now—without spending anything. You can, in fact, get started tracking an asset you already have—your website. Just install Google Analytics, Google's free web-traffic monitoring tool, on your website. It's a simple process, and it will provide all types of data about your website's visitors using a multitude of metrics and traffic sources to generate the results.

While Google Analytics isn't as robust as a commercial program designed for more extensive use, you can use it to extract long-term data, reveal trends, and obtain other valuable information. It will enable you to make wise, data-driven decisions that are thorough and revealing. Pretty amazing for a system that costs you nothing.

For instance, it tracks and analyzes website visitor behavior—such as where traffic is coming from, how audiences engage with your site, and how long visitors stay on a website (known as bounce rates), or on each page. This information alone will enable you to make better decisions that help make your website better meet your goals.

Another excellent use for this free program is analyzing social-media traffic. This will allow you to make changes to your social media–marketing campaigns based on what is and what isn't working best. You can also study mobile visitor traffic and patterns of usage, which can also help you extract information about customers who browse your site using their mobile devices. This will enable you to provide a better mobile experience that leads to more sales for you.

I hope it's clear to you by now that big data won't just help you make better business decisions; it can also help you predict the future! From the trends you identify, you can start to understand customer behavior and sales trends and predict behavioral models by extracting valuable information for future marketing campaigns. It can also help you discover the most opportune product recommendations and purchase histories, uncover email behaviors, and provide other invaluable metrics.

With this kind of solid data, businesses of all sizes can now better create personalized offers, track customer responses, and launch improved outreach campaigns.

12:00 A.M.

Do Your Customers and Employees Know What You're Thinking?

> "Regardless of the changes in technology, the market for well-crafted messages will always have an audience."
>
> —STEVE BURNETT, FOUNDER OF THE BURNETT GROUP

It's always important to keep people buzzing about what you do. This includes your own employees. The key to driving sales today is making the market for your products or services aware of who you are and letting them know that your offer can make their lives better. Better communications with your employees will make it easier for them to act as an extension of you to your customers.

I'm constantly amazed by the lack of communication skills exhibited by so many business owners and senior managers. Do your clients, customers, and your employees really know what you're thinking? Do they know what's current and happening at the company? Do you share stories and insights with them? Do you stop and have real and sincere conversations with employees of all levels in your company throughout the day?

I thought I did, but I was naive. I found out that I didn't. I also found that when you say nothing, employees will begin to think negative thoughts—or they stop thinking altogether. For example, at our annual reviews, I asked our people for an honest assessment of me. I said, "Don't hold back—I've already issued your bonus check for the year!"

I wasn't at all prepared for an issue that was brought to my attention by one of the employees in our order entry department. She said that I walked very quickly throughout the office with my head down. Because of this common behavior, she felt threatened by me and was even afraid to greet me as I walked by—although it was never my intention to create that kind of aura. I was very appreciative of her for speaking up and helping me grow into a better manager.

Quality two-way communication with your team is a requirement for small business success. You all have to be on the same page—or the whole book, metaphorically speaking, falls apart.

Here are some suggestions for creating better communications within your organization. These steps will help improve your communications and possibly bring more sales from your clients, prospects, and vendors. They'll also keep all your employees working with you and on the same page.

Blogging

Blogging is vitally important to most businesses today. Customers now expect the companies they do business with to have a blog. They appreciate getting to know the people they're buying from and possibly even contributing their own opinions and experiences to the site, perhaps helping the company better serve their needs in the process.

Everyone loves feeling that they're a part of something bigger than themselves. Your employees will feel a part of your team when they see your blog, and your clients and customers will feel they're "in the fold," too.

Just think about Harley Davidson owners for a moment. They're like members of a clan or—to use the business term for it—a "tribe." The members of this tribe are so proud of belonging, they'll often get a Harley Davidson tattoo, permanently marking their bodies to show their love of the brand. Hugh Hefner pulled this off with his Playboy empire, too. How many playboy bunny tattoos have you seen? I lost count.

You might never build this level of customer fanaticism, but a blog is one way to definitely let your customers, clients, and employees into the "inner sanctum" of your business, making them feel they're all a part of what you do.

A blog is also easy to set up. The technology to do so is free. There's really just time involved . . . and possibly a bit of money if you want to hire someone who does some of the setup or writing on your blog for you.

Show 'Em Your "Whoops!"

One of the best things you can do with a company blog is to share the occasional story about a mistake you made, pointing out to your readers what it taught you. People love knowing you're human and just as vulnerable as they are to errors . . . unless you're a brain surgeon or airline pilot. They'll love hearing what you learned, too, because they know this usually leads to an improvement in your services or product offerings down the line.

The only thing better than traffic to a blog is repeat traffic.

Do your clients or the industry you're in suffer from some common beliefs that are simply wrong? Debunk them in a blog post or—if you're up it—record a short podcast that is available to blog visitors.

The rewards of doing this right—even if you try and don't get it right all the time—are tremendous. Remember this: the biggest fear anyone has when it comes to being themselves is that it might make people not like them. Get over it. You'll never get everyone to like you anyway—and trying to be liked by everyone is one way I know of making sure no one likes you.

Building a solid blog for your business will provide a central "landing pad" for customers and future potential business—and it will enable you to easily reach out and engage with your customers and employees like nothing else can.

I could go on and on about blogs here, so I'm done now.

Email Newsletters

Another simple vehicle for communication is a monthly newsletter or quick weekly email—both would be even better—discussing successes and issues for the prior week or month in your business.

Make sure you set up at least one opt-in list for visitors; this way, you can directly reach potential new customers to join your tribe. These communications will continue to build your relationship and enable you to make special offers that can increase sales almost immediately whenever you hit that "send" button.

Polls and Surveys

You'll quickly find that people love participating in polls and surveys as much as you'll love the data and direction for your business they can provide. It always makes people feel important to be asked what they think. It also gives them more of a sense of belonging, as if being your customers makes them members of a special tribe or family.

CONCLUSION

Pass the Bowl of Serial

> "Timing, perseverance, and ten years
> of trying will eventually make you look
> like an overnight success."
>
> —BIZ STONE, COFOUNDER OF TWITTER

That's it—the story of my many forays into the world of small business and entrepreneurship. For those of you who stayed with me until the end, thank you. You've placed yourself into a very select, elite group of individuals by reading this far. You're one of the brave ones! You now "get it" that there will always be a risk to whatever you choose to do for a living. You also see that working for someone else places the odds of that risk into someone else's hands, rather than your own. You understand, as a result, that the sky's the limit when you take things into your own hands.

Despite all my warnings and some of the horror stories I've shared with you during our time together, you're ready to jump in with both feet and beat the odds your way. I applaud your decision. Most people will never fully realize how brave you are to have made the decision to forge ahead. I most certainly do.

Welcome aboard! The entire economy of the world needs you. There's a lot of work cut out for you. And long hours. Pursuing this dream is tough. But you know this going in and you're better prepared.

As much as I've enjoyed our time together, I do need to wrap this up, so I'll end our discussion with a warning. Take it from me, firsthand: beware of the serial entrepreneur bug. Once it bites you, it can take hold and never seems to let go.

I should know. That's where I live!

Just do me a huge favor. Don't let this great conversation die. Whatever you decide to do, you don't have to go it alone if we just stay in touch. I'll help any way I can. I also know a lot of other people who made it this far and will be happy to help, too. We can keep exchanging tips and information, and I'll let you in on any new developments in our select club.

After all, we're "inner circle" now. We know each other far better than most of the other contacts who come and go through our lives. We also share a dream—and the determination—to figure out the best way to reach it. There's no law stating that mavericks must be loners. Together, we can enhance our capabilities exponentially.

Now you know a lot about me, I look forward to getting to know you! Please visit www.jeffshavitz.com, and let's stay in touch. I also encourage you to visit www.trafficjamming.com, my current business, and become a TrafficJammer to help your company grow more successfully. TrafficJamming is a membership club to help business owners and entrepreneurs grow their companies more successfully to maximize profitability and realize their dreams. Good luck!

About the Author

Jeff Shavitz is a successful entrepreneur. He worked as an investment banker at Lehman Brothers in the Corporate Finance/Mergers and Acquisitions Group, specializing in transactions ranging from $250MM–$500MM. With an offer in hand to attend graduate school to earn his MBA and continue his climb up the corporate ladder, Jeff consciously decided to leave this fast-paced, well-paying position to start up a one-person business. Friends said, "What is he thinking?"

A passion for creating "a life of his own" was the driving force in determining Jeff's business future. Out of his New York apartment, while still working on Wall Street, he created "Spectoculars," a branded paper-folding binocular that received an NFL license in 1991. At Super Bowl XXX, 250,000 pairs were distributed.

Fast-forward several years and Jeff cofounded Charge Card Systems Inc., a national credit card processing company that helps merchants with their processing requirements, including the acceptance of Visa, MasterCard, American Express, and Discover. The company grew to more than 700 sales agents throughout the country with three regional offices. In 2012, Jeff and his partners sold the business to Card Connect, owned by private equity firm FTV Capital. The purchase was the company's largest acquisition to date.

The culmination of Jeff's past experiences with the small and mid-size business owners is TrafficJamming LLC (www.traffic jamming.com), a membership association for business owners and entrepreneurs. All businesses want more traffic—in essence, traffic means sales. TrafficJamming provides its members with a destination website filled with information, technology tools, and insights to help grow your business. TrafficJamming is not a buying club or traditional business group, but rather a modern organization to help executives realize their professional dreams. Among its many services, TrafficJamming provides proven and cutting-edge technology solutions to help build awareness of our members' products and services—with the ultimate goal of building a loyal tribe of clients.

In addition to his first book, *Size Doesn't Matter: Why Small Business Is Big Business*, Jeff has also published *Small Business AhaMessages*, a collection of 140 key axioms that every business owner should consider when starting or running their companies. His third book, *The Power of Residual Income: You Can Bank On It*, which educates business owners on the power of residual and recurring income versus transactional income.

Jeff received his Bachelor of Arts degree in Economics from Tufts University and spent one semester at the London School of Economics, specializing in finance. He is very active in numerous charitable and civic community organizations and business groups, including Young Presidents' Organization.

He is married and has two daughters, a son, and two dogs. Besides being with family, enjoying good health, and living to see worldwide peace, Jeff's selfish goal is to play the 100 top golf courses in the United States.

To learn more about the author, visit www.JeffShavitz.com or contact him at jeff@trafficjamming.com or 800-878-4100.

CPSIA information can be obtained at www.ICGtesting.com
Printed in the USA
BVOW02s0354060915

416768BV00009B/137/P